TRUTH
FOR
ALL
TIME

Hallelujah!

Exploring and enjoying the
Old Testament benedictions

Stan K Evers

Day One

ENDORSEMENTS

It is a real pleasure to commend Hallelujah!, *the latest offering from the pen of Stan Evers. As its subtitle helpfully alerts us, this is an invitation to explore and enjoy the benedictions of the Old Testament. In other words, this is not intended to be a deeply technical work. Rather, its chief aim is twofold: to encourage the reader to a better understanding of these benedictions, and also to inspire a personal and devotional response to them. In this it succeeds admirably, and in no small measure due to the warmth of a pastoral heart which pervades each of its chapters.*

Hallelujah! *is a worthy companion to the author's earlier work on the New Testament entitled* Doxology! *Both volumes are available from Day One Publications.*

Daniel Webber, former Mission Director of the European Missionary Fellowship and Principal of its School of Biblical Studies for 21 years. Before joining the EMF he had served as pastor of Waterford House Evangelical Free Church, Strood, Kent. He now lives in Bangor, Northern Ireland.

Benedictions and doxologies, which often conclude sections and passages of Holy Scripture, are all too frequently overlooked by even the most attentive of Bible readers. But as this new study by Stan Evers rightly reminds us, these portions of God's Word contain doctrinal riches well worth contemplating and thrilling assurances we need to remember. Read, ponder well, and rejoice!

Michael A. G. Haykin, FRHistS, Professor of Church History, The Southern Baptist Theological Seminary, Louisville, Kentucky

© Day One Publications 2019

ISBN 978-1-84625-665-3

All Scripture quotations, unless stated otherwise, are from the
anglicized edition of the ESV Bible copyright © 2002 Collins, part
of HarperCollins Publishers.

British Library Cataloguing in Publication Data available

Published by Day One Publications
Ryelands Road, Leominster, HR6 8NZ
Telephone 01568 613 740 FAX 01568 611 473
email—sales@dayone.co.uk
web site—www.dayone.co.uk

Cover design by Kathryn Chedgzoy
Printed by 4Edge

In loving memory of Maureen (1938–2014).
We were married for 36 years.

Contents

After the publication of *Doxology! Exploring and enjoying the New Testament benedictions* (2012), the Day One editors asked me to write a follow-up book about Old Testament doxologies and benedictions. I am sorry for the long delay. Meanwhile, I've been encouraged by feedback from readers. Thank you!

I began *Doxology!* with two simple definitions: a benediction is a prayer and a doxology is praise. Benedictions are sometimes praise and a doxology is often a prayer. However, I would suggest that prayer is more prominent in benediction and praise more prominent in doxology. I will follow the same definitions in this book. I also explained that 'benediction' comes from two Latin words that mean 'to speak well of', and that 'doxology' is derived from the Greek word for 'glory'.

Psalm 134 is a short but interesting psalm because it combines both benediction and doxology: 'Come, bless the Lord' (v. 1)—doxology—'May the Lord bless you' (v. 3)—benediction. What is the difference between our blessing God and his blessing us? 'Motyer helpfully puts it like this: "When he 'blesses' he reviews our needs and meets them; when we bless him we review his excellencies and worship him."'[1]

While planning this book it soon became evident that the abundance of Old Testament doxologies and benedictions is overwhelming. Careful selection was essential so as to keep to a reasonable length. I pray that my choice will be useful to you.

Thank you to David Preston, Michael Haykin, Mostyn Roberts and Daniel Webber for reading the manuscript, and for making many helpful suggestions. Most of all I thank Wendy, my wife, for her encouragement. Several times I've discussed matters with her relating to grammar. Her proof-reading skills have proved invaluable.

May our thinking about the Old Testament doxologies and benedictions lead to a fresh awareness of God's grace and glory! He is a mighty God worthy of our praise!

Preface

NOTES

1   Quoted by Philip Eveson, *Psalms*, vol. 2 (Welwyn Commentary, Welwyn Garden City, 2015), p.420.

Calling on God's name

At that time people began to call upon the name of the LORD. (Gen. 4:26)

Abenediction is prayer and a doxology is praise—two essential aspects of worship. When did people begin to pray to, and to praise, God? To answer this inquiry we turn to Genesis, which is the book of origins.

We read in Genesis that after Adam and Eve had eaten the forbidden fruit they felt guilty and were ashamed; therefore, they 'hid themselves from the presence of the LORD God among the trees of the garden.' Then the encounter they feared takes place: 'They heard the sound of the LORD God walking in the garden in the cool of the day' (Gen. 3:8). This verse implies that God's evening walk was an everyday occurrence. Prior to their fall into sin Adam and Eve enjoyed daily fellowship with God; they looked forward to this precious time with their Creator. How could God who is a spirit (John 4:24) and therefore has no body walk each evening in the Garden of Eden? This is what theologians call a 'theophany'—an appearance of Jesus Christ on earth before his birth at Bethlehem.[1]

God, who is good and kind, had warned Adam and Eve that 'In the day that you eat of it ['the tree of the knowledge of good and evil'] you shall surely die' (Gen. 2:17). Notice the words, 'In the day'—spiritual death was immediate though physical death did not take place until many years later. There was now a breach in their fellowship with God. Sin entered the world. God banished Adam and Eve from Eden, but did not destroy them. Nonetheless, the gracious God gave them a promise of a coming Saviour: 'I will put enmity between you [the serpent] and the woman, and between your offspring and her offspring; he shall bruise your head, and you shall bruise his heel' (Gen. 3:15). This first gospel promise points to

Jesus Christ dying in the place of sinners at Calvary. To defeat Satan, who came into Eden in the guise of a serpent, Christ was bruised (Isaiah 53:4–5). Perhaps we have an anticipation of Christ's death in the fact that God clothed guilty Adam and Eve in the skins of animals (Gen. 3:21). It seems probable that the animals offered were sacrifices to appease the holy God.

Turning from chapter 3 to chapter 4 we read the earliest account of people meeting for worship: 'At that time people began to call upon the name of the LORD' (Gen. 4:26). To 'call upon the name of the LORD' is used in the book of Genesis to indicate the worship of God and is sometimes associated with sacrifices. For example, when Abraham moved to Bethel 'he built an altar to the LORD and called upon the name of the LORD' (Gen. 12:8), and when he returned to Bethel where 'he had made an altar … Abram called upon the name of the LORD' (Gen. 13:4).

Let's pose some questions to unwrap Genesis 4:26.

Question 1: When did people call on the Lord?

Moses, the author of Genesis, informs us that public worship started 'at that time', and the context fills out these three words.

We read in Genesis 4:20–23 about *the advance of civilisation*. These verses list the children of the two wives of Lamech. Lamech was a bad role model for his sons, Jabal, Jubal and Tubal-cain, and his daughter Naamah. 'Here was a father of shepherds and a father of musicians, but not a father of the faithful. Here was one to teach in brass and iron, but none to teach the good knowledge of the Lord. Here were devices on how to be rich and how to be mighty, and how to be merry, but nothing of God.'[2] The world has not changed! People today are busy with their lives and consider God as irrelevant. Believers are to encourage one another to love and obey God in evil days. We do this as we enjoy fellowship with God and his people. We are to shine as lights in the darkness (Phil. 2:15).

We also read in Genesis 4 about the *spread of evil*. Sin spread like a disease into the bloodstream of the human race after Adam's sin. We see evidence of this fact in Cain's murder of his brother Abel. Cain was angry with God and with his brother. Why? Both brothers brought offerings to the Lord. Abel brought 'the firstborn of the flock', which implies that the animal died instead of Abel. Cain brought 'the fruit of the ground', which was the result of his own hard work. He rejected God's way of worship—the blood of an animal shed instead of the sinner—therefore, God rejected his offering (Gen. 4:1–16).

Philip Eveson, a former Principal of the London Seminary, comments: 'It is clear that Cain and Abel knew more about offerings than the text suggests. We are only given the minimum of information, but Moses wishes us to read these early incidents of sacrifice in the light of later revelation.'[3] We may add to this Wayne Grudem's remark: 'The fact that the first two children of Adam and Eve, Cain and Abel, offered sacrifices to the Lord (Gen.4:3–4) indicates their consciousness of a need to make some kind of payment for the guilt of their sin, and of God's promise of acceptance of sacrifices offered in the right way.'[4]

The writer to the Hebrews uses Abel as an illustration of faith (Heb. 11:4) because he obeyed God's command to offer a blood sacrifice. Quoting again from Hebrews we read: 'Without the shedding of blood there is no forgiveness of sins' (Heb. 9:22). This is a principle enshrined in Jewish worship in the tabernacle and later in the temple. Now God accepts only those who come to him through Christ the Lamb of God (John 1:29).

We have further evidence of the spread of evil in the conduct of Lamech, who was a descendant of Cain and the first bigamist (Gen. 4:19). This was a deliberate act of defiance against God, who had commanded that one man should marry only one wife and that the two would become 'one flesh' (Gen. 2:24; Matt.19:3–9; Eph. 5:31). Besides this sinfulness, Lamech boasts that he had killed a man in self-defence; but he feels no guilt or remorse (Gen. 4:23–24). Killing a young man who wounded him is excessive revenge. While Lamech praised himself, the godly praised God.

Two births are associated with the beginning of worship: the birth of Seth (Gen. 4:25–26), whose name means 'appointed one', a son for Adam and Eve; and the birth of their grandson, Enosh, whose name means 'weak and frail'. Adam was 130 years old when Seth was born and lived another 800 years (Gen. 5:3–5). Seth was 105 years old when Enosh was born (Gen. 5:6). Eve's use of the term 'offspring' ('seed', NKJV) looks back to the promise of Genesis 3:15. Eveson writes: 'Eve was aware that God was remembering his promise. She was looking forward to a special "seed" [Gal. 3:15–16]. The whole of Genesis is taken up with developing this theme of a particular family line.' He adds, 'While Cain and his descendants were setting up their humanistic city, another city, a heavenly one, was developing. People were being brought together for the first time for public worship. This worship was associated with Seth, who replaced Abel. There is no indication, however, that the calling on God was confined to the descendants of Seth.'[5] From the descendants of Seth came Jesus, the Messiah who saves sinners who call on his name for salvation.

Question 2: Who called on the name of the Lord?

Moses tells us: 'At that time *people* began to call upon the name of the LORD' (Gen. 4:26)—but which people?

- God's people, such as Adam and Eve, Abel, Seth and Enosh, and those listed below, worshipped God. These people are described as 'the sons of God', though sadly, they began to marry 'the daughters of man', a term used to describe those who were not worshippers of the true God (Gen. 6:1–4).
- And later people like Enoch, who 'walked with God' (Gen. 5:24).
- People like Noah, who was 'a righteous man, blameless in his generation' (Gen. 6:9). What was his 'generation' like? Read

Genesis 6:5–13 to find out! Noah found favour because of God's grace.

- People like Abraham, who obeyed God's call to leave his family and country because he believed God's promise that through him the Lord would bless the world, a promise fulfilled in Christ. It's clear that Abraham looked beyond earthly Canaan to an eternal homeland in heaven (Heb. 11:8–16).

We could go through the Bible adding the names of people who worshipped God. None of the people mentioned were sinless; but they loved God and sought to serve him despite the wickedness of men and women around them. God's grace is greater than our sin! Are you a Christian? Then you may add your name to the people who call on the name of the Lord!

Question 3: On whom did the people call?

We read that '... people began to call on *the name of the LORD*.' This is the first time that we read in the Bible that God's name is 'LORD'. This name was explained more fully when God spoke to Moses from the burning bush. The 'LORD' is the 'I AM WHO I AM' (Exod. 3:14) –Jehovah/Yahweh, the eternally present covenant God who heard the cries of his enslaved people. He said: 'I have surely seen the affliction of my people who are in Egypt and have heard their cry because of their taskmasters. I know their sufferings, and I have come down to deliver them … and to bring them up out of that land to … a land flowing with milk and honey' (Exod. 3:7–8). This God walked on earth in a human body (Col. 1:19; 2:9). While on earth 'He was despised and rejected by men; a man of sorrows and acquainted with grief' (Isa. 53:3). Now enthroned in heaven he is our great high priest who sympathises with us and from whom we 'receive mercy and find grace to help in time of need' (Heb. 4:14–16).

The mention of 'the name' (Gen. 4:26) indicates all that God has revealed about himself in the Bible. When we have sinned we call on the God of grace to forgive us; when we need guidance we call on God our heavenly Father to lead us; when we are weak we call on the all-powerful God for strength; when we are troubled we call on the God of comfort to be near us; when we are dying we call on the gracious God to receive us.

We read in Genesis 21:33 that Abraham 'called there on the name of the LORD, the Everlasting God.' God never dies! We may call on him in all circumstances and at all times in our life.

Have you called on the Lord?

A prophet named Joel and an apostle named Paul wrote about calling on the name of the Lord: 'Everyone who calls on the name of the LORD shall be saved' (Joel 2:32; Rom. 10:13). 'Everyone'—put your name in the text—have *you* called on the Lord to save you from sin? Call on him *today*!

NOTES

1 See my book *Christ in Exodus* (London: Grace Publications Trust, 2010), pp.28–30.

2 John Currid, *Genesis*, vol. 1 (EP Study Commentary; Darlington: Evangelical Press, 2003), p.154.

3 Philip Eveson, *The Book of Origins* (Welwyn Commentary; Darlington: Evangelical Press, 2001), p.118.

4 Wayne Grudem, *Systematic Theology: an Introduction to Biblical Doctrine* (Leicester: Inter-Varsity Press, 1994), p.118.

5 Eveson, *The Book of Origins*, pp.130–131.

A grandfather's benediction

Jacob blessed Joseph and said … God … bless the boys. (Gen. 48:15–16)

Children and grandchildren ought to thank God for the godly lives and daily prayers of parents and grandparents. How easy to take these blessings for granted! Jacob is an example of a grandfather blessing his grandchildren (Gen. 48) and a parent blessing his children (Gen. 49).

The patriarch Jacob, age 147, who had lived seventeen years in Egypt and was near death, blesses his grandsons, Manasseh and Ephraim, the sons of Joseph (Gen. 48:20; 47:28). He remembers the time when 'God Almighty' (Gen. 48:3) blessed him at Luz (Bethel) (see Gen. 35:1–15): 'I will make you fruitful and multiply you, and I will make of you a company of peoples and will give this land to your offspring after you for an everlasting possession' (Gen. 48:4). These words echo those of his father Isaac (Gen. 28:1–5). At the end of his life Jacob owned only the burial cave near Shechem which he purchased from the sons of Hamor (Gen. 33:18–20). His grandfather Abraham had already bought a burial place for his wife Sarah (Gen. 23). Between them the patriarchs owned only two small pieces of land; nevertheless, they believed that God would keep his word. The words 'fruitful and multiply' (Gen. 48:4) are reminiscent of the original creation mandate (Gen. 1:28). By recalling these promises Jacob encouraged Joseph 'not to look to possessions in Egypt … but to set his sights on the divine promises and the heavenly inheritance.'[1] This was the 'everlasting possession' which God promised to Jacob (Gen. 48:4). We too are to 'look not to the things that are seen but to the things that are unseen. For the things that are seen are transient, but the things that are unseen are eternal' (2 Cor. 4:18). This treasure is more valuable than any inheritance we may leave our children!

'God Almighty' (Gen. 48:3) translates the Hebrew 'El Shaddai', which means 'the God who is all-sufficient'. This gracious God let Jacob see not only his son, whose supposed death had caused inconsolable grief, but also to see his two grandchildren, whom he kissed and embraced (Gen. 48:9–10). It was El Shaddai who sustained him in the loss of Rachel, his dearly-loved wife (Gen. 48:7). El Shaddai reassured Jacob when he was afraid of travelling to Egypt (Gen. 46:1–4). He would have known that in an earlier famine the Lord had specifically forbidden his father Isaac 'to go down to Egypt', telling him instead to remain in the Promised Land (Gen. 26:1–5). The decision to leave was surely traumatic. He was aged 130 when he undertook this long journey (Gen. 47:7–10). El Shaddai would be with him as he faced the reality of death (Gen. 48:1, 21). God walks with us in the varying circumstances of our lives.

How does the old patriarch face death? He focuses on the future rather than on his physical problems (Gen. 48:1). Blessing Joseph's sons was an expression of his faith in God: 'By faith Jacob, when dying, blessed each of the sons of Joseph, bowing in worship over the head of his staff' (Heb. 11:21). His frail body needed the support of his staff but his confidence in God was strong. Because, like his grandfather Abraham, he looked forward to an eternal city, he had no fear of death (Heb. 11:10–16). Jacob's descendant Jesus Christ died and rose again to conquer death.

God's choice

Jacob desired that God who had blessed him would also bless his grandsons Manasseh and Ephraim, 'Bring them to me, please, that I may bless them' (Gen. 48:9). Both sons were born before the famine and shared an Egyptian mother, but this did not disqualify them from the blessing (Gen. 41:50–51). Jacob adopted the two boys, probably in their late teens, as his own sons (Gen. 48:5–6). Eveson explains the significance of this: 'Ephraim and Manasseh suddenly became joint-heirs along with all their uncles of the promises made to Abraham and were treated as Jacob's first-born sons (see 1 Chr. 5:1–2). They became tribes in their own right alongside the other eleven. In this way, Joseph was honoured by Jacob.'[2] It was through his sons that 'Joseph received a double share in the land of promise and a place of prominence.'[3] After adopting Joseph's sons Jacob recalls the early death of Rachel, mother of Benjamin (Gen. 48:7), which meant that he was unable to have further children by her. 'Adopting Joseph's children made up for his loss.'[4] 'From his knees' (Gen. 48:12) means 'beside his knees' (NKJV) and was part of the legal rite of adoption.

The question, 'Whose are these?' (Gen. 48:8) means that the nearly-blind Jacob wanted to be sure that the boys were Joseph's sons. This query also directs us back to chapter 27, where we read that his own father Isaac was in a similar position when Jacob deceived him and stole the blessing of the first-born. 'In the present episode, once again the first-born will not receive the blessing—but this time it is the patriarch who causes the unexpected to occur.' What is Joseph's response to the adoption of his sons? Verse 12 tells us. 'Joseph, the second most powerful man in Egypt, responded gratefully and respectfully by prostrating himself before his father.'[5]

It was because of Jacob's failing sight that Joseph places Manasseh, the firstborn, nearest to his father's right hand and Ephraim, the younger, toward his left hand. The firstborn inherited special privileges along with extra responsibilities in a Jewish family. However, Jacob places his right hand, the symbol of power and pre-eminence, on the head of the younger rather than the elder. When Joseph tries to take his father's right hand and rest it on Manasseh, he refuses to let his son move his hands. Placing his right hand on Ephraim was not the mistake of a feeble old man who was almost blind; it was an indication of God's choice (Gen. 48:13–14, 17–19). Jacob's words, 'I know, my son, I know' (v. 19), reveal that he 'sees into the future with great clarity. He sees that Manasseh will become a great people, but Ephraim an even greater one.'[6]

Just as God chose Abel instead of Cain, and just as he chose Isaac, Jacob's father, instead of his older brother, Ishmael, and just as he chose Jacob instead of Esau, the firstborn, so God chose Joseph's younger son Ephraim. It was through Ephraim's descendants that the Lord would keep the promise of verse 19: 'He [Manasseh] also shall become a people, and he also shall be great. Nevertheless, his younger brother shall be greater than he, and his offspring shall become a multitude of nations.' The apostle Paul uses God's choice of Jacob, the younger, rather than Esau, his older brother, as an illustration of divine sovereignty in salvation (Rom. 9:10–13).

Perhaps we may see in Jacob's crossing his hands and transferring the blessing to the younger son a picture of what God did when Jesus, God's firstborn, died on the cross? The Father transferred our sins to his Son; he transferred the righteousness of Christ to us. He treats the believer as his firstborn! Ephraim did not deserve his grandfather's blessing; we do not merit God's blessing. Jacob's blessing came to his adopted sons; so God blesses us his adopted children (Eph. 1:3–6).

God's promises

God's promise in verse 4—'I will make of you a company of peoples' —and in verse 19—'his offspring shall become a multitude of nations'— and Jacob's blessing in verse 16—'Let them grow into a multitude in the midst of the earth'—find their ultimate fulfilment in Christ. It was from Jacob's twelve sons that the nation of Israel emerged, and it was from that nation, in the Promised Land of Canaan, that the Saviour of the world was born. These promises anticipated the elect of God, a vast number comprising Jews and non-Jews, coming from all the nations of the world (Rev. 7:9–10).

God the shepherd

Jacob's blessing is in two parts: the first addressed to Joseph (Gen. 48:15–16), and the second part addressed to his grandsons (Gen. 48:20).

WALKING WITH GOD (GEN. 48:15).

Jacob's grandfather, Abraham, and his father, Isaac, were men who, like Noah and Enoch, walked with God (Gen. 5:22–24; 6:9). They enjoyed personal fellowship with God. Jacob too had walked with God for many years. 'Walking with God' indicates not only fellowship but obedience. Those honoured with God's favour were obliged to live a life that pleased him.

As Christians we understand more about God and enjoy deeper fellowship with him than the patriarchs, because the Lord walked on earth. He is Immanuel, who lived in a human body (Matt. 1:23; Col. 1:19; 2:9). It is through his atoning death that we have access to God (Heb. 10:19). We look forward to God, who walked with Adam and Eve in Eden (Gen. 3:8), walking with his people on the new earth. The apostle John saw 'the holy city, new Jerusalem, coming down out of heaven from God, prepared as a bride adorned for her husband'—the city/ bride is the church. John continues, 'Behold, the dwelling place of God is with man. He will dwell with them, and they will be his people, and God himself will be with them as their God' (Rev.21:1–3).

FOLLOWING THE SHEPHERD (GEN. 48:15).

Jacob, who had spent his life shepherding, spoke about 'the God who has been my shepherd all my life long to this day' (Gen. 48:15; 46:31–34; 47:3–4). This is the first reference in the Bible to God as the shepherd of his people. The next time this description is given is in connection with the patriarch's blessing of his son (Gen. 49:24). Too often Jacob was like an erring sheep; but the divine shepherd cared for him as his provider, protector and guide. Jacob calls the shepherd 'God': the Hebrew is

Elohim, the all-powerful creator God who guided and defended the patriarch (Gen. 48:15). God the shepherd never abandons his sheep! Christ the good Shepherd died to give them eternal life: therefore, not one will perish because they are secure in his nail-pierced hands (John 10:10, 28–30).

THE REDEEMING ANGEL (GEN. 48:16).

The angel is 'the Angel of the LORD': the pre-incarnate Son of God, who appeared several times in the Old Testament.[7] This Angel appeared to Jacob three times: at Bethel (Gen. 28:13), in Paddan-aram (Gen. 31:11, 13) and at Peniel (Gen. 32:23–30). At Peniel he identifies this Angel as God, 'So Jacob called the name of the place Peniel, saying, "For I have seen God face to face, and yet my life has been delivered"' (Gen. 32:30). Peniel means 'the face of God'. God's holy Son wrestling with sinful Jacob was a turning point in the patriarch's life.

This angel is 'the redeeming angel'. This is the first occurrence of redemption terminology in the Bible. This word 'redeeming' refers to the kinsman-redeemer, a next of kin who stepped in to rescue a relative in trouble (Lev. 25:23–34). We have an example of this in the book of Ruth. Boaz bought back land belonging to Naomi's late husband Elimelech and his sons Chilion and Mahlon, who had married Ruth. To redeem the land Boaz had to marry Ruth. God redeemed his people from bondage in Egypt (Exod. 15:13). Christ is our kinsman-redeemer whose blood purchased us in order to set us from free from sin, Satan, the curse of the law and the fear of death (Gal. 3:13; Eph. 1:7; 1 Peter 1:18–19; Heb. 2:14–15).

It is this God—the divine angel and the kinsman-redeemer—that Jacob prays will 'bless the boys', a prayer that they would know the blessings the covenant God had made with his family (Gen. 48:16). It was because of God's blessing that during the wilderness wanderings the tribes of Ephraim and Manasseh numbered 72,700 adult males (Num.

1:32–35). After the division of the nation (930 BC) Ephraim takes on the leadership of the ten northern tribes of Israel. The remaining two tribes formed the southern tribe of Judah. We too, like aged Jacob, may pray for God to bless our children and grandchildren, especially with the gift of salvation.

We read about Jacob's death and burial in the next chapter (49:28–33). He died praising God and praying for his children and grandchildren. 'It's a good thing to be able to end your life knowing you've completed God's business the way he wanted it done.'[8]

Chapter 2

NOTES

1 Philip Eveson, *The Book of Origins* (Welwyn Commentary; Darlington: Evangelical Press, 2001), p.552.

2 Eveson, *The Book of Origins*, p.553.

3 Eveson, *The Book of Origins*, p.553.

4 John Currid, *Genesis*, vol. 2 (EP Study Commentary; Darlington: Evangelical Press, 2003), p.365.

5 Eveson, *The Book of Origins*, p.554.

6 Currid, *Genesis*, p.368.

7 These appearances of God are known as 'theophanies.' I have listed them in Appendix 2, *Christ in Exodus* (London: Grace Publications Trust, 2010), pp.148–150.

8 Warren Wiersbe, *Be Authentic—Exhibiting Real Faith in a Real World, Genesis 25–50* (ebook; Eastbourne: David C. Cook UK, Kingsway Communications. First published Wheaton, Illinois: Victor Books, 1997).

Moses' song of praise

I will sing to the LORD, for he has triumphed gloriously … The LORD will reign for ever and ever. (Exod. 15:1, 18)

Imagine the spontaneous singing of over two million people praising God, led by Moses and his sister Miriam, accompanied by tambourines and the sound of the dancing feet of women. This is the scene in Exodus 15 where we read the first song recorded in the Bible. The Israelites' song expresses their amazement and exhilaration after safely crossing the Red Sea.

This exuberant song of praise divides into four stanzas: verses 1–5; 6–10; 11–13 and 14–17. Stanzas one and two end with the words, 'they went down into the depths like a stone' (v. 5) and 'they sank like lead in the mighty waters' (v. 10), emphasising the finality of the enemy army's overthrow. The other two stanzas conclude with a reference to God's 'holy abode' (v. 13) and 'the sanctuary' of the 'LORD' (v. 17). The song concludes with an affirmation: 'The LORD will reign for ever and ever' (v. 18). The focus of Moses' song is clearly 'The LORD' who is the redeemer of his people.

What do we learn about the Lord from Moses' song?

The Lord's covenant

Moses' doxology begins with the words: 'I will sing to the LORD' (v. 1). The word 'LORD' occurs thirteen times in verses 1–21. This name points back to Exodus 3, to the time when Jehovah the 'I AM WHO I AM' spoke to Moses from the burning bush. He is the eternal and unchanging God who heard the cries of his enslaved people and remembered his covenant—his promise—(Exodus 2:23–25; 3:7–10) to give Abraham a land in which the

Messiah-Saviour would be born. God also promised that Abraham's descendants would be more numerous than the stars, a promise fulfilled in Christ. He blessed the whole world through Abraham.[1] The spiritual children of Abraham are those who have the faith of Abraham (Gal. 3:7–9).

To keep his promises God delivered his people from Egypt and brought them through the Red Sea. To keep his promises he drowned Pharaoh's army in that same sea. The God who cared for the Hebrews cares for us too.

The Exodus was as an act of redemption: 'You have led in your steadfast love the people whom you have redeemed' (v. 13). The phrase 'the greatness of your arm' (v. 16) recalls Exodus 6:6, where we read: 'I am the LORD, and I will bring you out from under the burdens of the Egyptians, and I will deliver you from slavery to them, and I will redeem you with an outstretched arm and with great acts of judgement.' The blood of the Passover Lamb was the price of redemption for Israel (Exod. 12). The blood of Christ, shed some 1,500 years later, was the price to redeem believers from the tyrant sin (1 Cor. 5:7; 1 Peter 1:18–19).

The Lord's triumph

Verse 2 picks up the word 'salvation' from the previous chapter: 'Moses said to the people, "Fear not, stand firm, and see the salvation of the LORD, which he will work for you today. For the Egyptians whom you see today, you shall never see again. The LORD will fight for you, and you have only to be silent"' (14:13–14).

It was not easy to remain calm with the ferocious Egyptian army rapidly advancing towards them and the insurmountable Red Sea in front of them! But God is the Almighty; he easily hurls Pharaoh's chariots like a stone into the sea (v. 1). The Egyptian officers sank like a stone as 'the floods covered them' (v. 5). It was the 'right hand' of the Lord who is 'glorious in power' which shattered 'the enemy' (v. 6). In Hebrew culture 'the right hand' was the symbol of power and strength.

The epithet 'my father's God' (v. 2) indicates the special relationship between God and Israel his chosen people. It also reminds us of Moses' faithfulness to God. He had not forsaken the God of his fathers. Now all God's people—believing Jews and Gentiles—belong to God's 'chosen race' and are 'a people for his own possession' (1 Peter 2:9). All believers are children of God through Jesus Christ. He is God's eternal Son; we are his children by adoption. Are we loyal to our divine Father? Do we, like Moses, delight to serve him?

The Lord who is 'a man of war' (v. 3) fought for Israel. He fights for us too! To quote Paul: 'If God is for us, who can be against us?' (Rom. 8:31). Our enemies are the world (unbelievers), the flesh (sin remaining in the regenerate heart) and the devil. Our weapons are the sword of God's Word and effective prayer (Eph. 6:10–20; James 5:16).

The Lord's uniqueness

The third stanza begins with a question: 'Who is like you, O LORD?' (v. 11). The defeat of Egypt at the Red Sea displays God's uniqueness. The enemy boasts: 'I will pursue, I will overtake, I will divide the spoil, my desire shall have its fill of them. I will draw my sword; my hand shall destroy them' (v. 9). Israel's enemies are like stubble that God easily burns (v. 7). He has merely to blast with his nostrils (v. 8) and blow with his mouth to humble the proud Egyptians (v. 10). 'God resists the proud but exalts the humble' is a motif that runs throughout the Bible (e.g. Prov. 3:34; James 4:6; 1 Peter 5:5).

The question: 'Who is like you, O LORD, among the gods?' (v. 11) does not imply that God is one among many gods; he is the only God who performs 'glorious deeds'; he alone could deliver his people from bondage. The gods of Egypt were powerless idols, but the true God is 'majestic in holiness, awesome in glorious deeds'. 'Yahweh [Jehovah] is majestic in his wholly otherness. He is like nothing else'.[2]

The Lord's love

Verse 12 opens with words similar to God's command to Moses: 'You stretched out your right hand.' Moses stretched out his hand and the sea divided so that the Israelites could walk through it (Exod. 14:16). It was God who really had the power to open and close the waters. The word 'swallowed' (v. 12) is reminiscent of Aaron's staff swallowing the rods of the Egyptian magicians (Exod. 7:8–13).

The miraculous crossing of the Red Sea spread terror among the nations (vv. 14–16). An example of this fear comes in the story of Rahab, who some forty years after the Exodus met the twelve Israelite spies. She said: 'We have heard how the LORD dried up the water of the Red Sea before you came out of Egypt … And as soon as we heard it, our hearts melted, and there was no spirit left in any man because of you, for the LORD your God, he is God in the heavens above and on the earth beneath' (Josh. 2:10–12). The Canaanites feared God but did not seek him for mercy. God spared only those in Rahab's house, identified by the scarlet cord, when he destroyed the wicked city of Jericho. Likewise, it is those who trust in Christ alone, whose red blood flowed at Calvary, that will escape God's wrath when he destroys this world by fire (2 Peter 3:10).

The Exodus, and God's subsequent provision in the wilderness, was not only a display of his power, but also an expression of his unfailing love for his people (v. 13). 'Steadfast love' means God's loyal love to Israel. He never failed them. He preserved them, and cared for them to fulfil his promise of a coming Messiah, the Saviour of the world. This God loves his church with an everlasting love (Jer. 31:3; Rom. 8:28–39).

What is the meaning of 'your holy abode' in verse 13? It may refer to Sinai, where God gave Moses the Law, or to the Promised Land. The church is now God's 'holy temple ... a dwelling place for God by the Spirit' (Eph. 2:21–22).

The Lord's reign

So Moses' jubilant song ends as it began, extolling the Lord, the eternal king. The Pharaohs who enslaved the Hebrews, and the Pharaoh whose army chased them to the Red Sea, are now dead. The mighty empires of Assyria, Babylon, Persia, Greece and Rome have long since disappeared. Communism in Russia, East Germany, and in Eastern European countries, collapsed in the twentieth century. The British Commonwealth has shrunk in size. But God's kingdom is never ending. Jehovah is the eternal King.

The song of Moses and of the Lamb

In Revelation 15, the aged apostle John hears echoes of Moses' ancient song. He writes in verses 2–3 of God's people playing harps and singing 'the song of Moses, the servant of God, and the song of the Lamb'. Why should the exiled John remind persecuted first-century believers of Moses' song? The mighty Saviour who drowned Pharaoh's army in the Red Sea would defend his tormented people and crush the Roman Empire. And why does John add 'the song of the Lamb' to 'the song of Moses'? Because the conquering Lord of the Exodus is the slain Lamb of Revelation. Thousands of angels and the 'great multitude' of the elect will sing eternally the Lamb's song, 'Worthy is the Lamb who was slain, to receive power and wealth and wisdom and might and honour and glory and blessing!' (Rev. 5:12; see also v. 13; 7:9–11). Even now on earth, whatever our temptations and trials, we may sing this song of the Lamb.

Chapter 3

NOTES

1   See Genesis 12:1–3; 17:1–8; 22:15–18.

2   John Currid, *Exodus*, vol. 1 (EP Study Commentary; Darlington: Evangelical Press, 2000), p.318.

A promise of peace

The LORD spoke to Moses, saying, 'Speak to Aaron and his sons, saying, Thus you shall bless the people of Israel: you shall say to them, The LORD bless you and keep you; the LORD make his face to shine upon you and be gracious to you; the LORD lift up his countenance upon you and give you peace. So shall they put my name upon the people of Israel, and I will bless them.' (Num. 6:22–27)

The storm is raging. The sea is beating against the rocks. The lightning is flashing, the thunder is roaring, the wind is blowing; but a little bird is sound asleep in the crevice of a rock with its head tucked serenely under its wing. It sleeps in the storm! Would you like peace in life's storms? God gives peace to those who trust him.[1] God promises peace in the benediction of Numbers 6.

This benediction, frequently used at the end of worship, finds an echo in several of the Psalms, such as, Psalm 67:1 and Psalm 134:3: 'May God be gracious to us and bless us and make his face to shine upon us'; 'May the LORD bless you from Zion, he who made heaven and earth!' The Aaronic benediction is arguably the most familiar passage in the book of Numbers. What is the meaning of the word 'bless'? 'To the Hebrew mind "blessing" was certain and specific, a vast store of priceless gifts which money could never buy. It included such treasures as human love, the gift of children, the joys of family life, the delight of home and the security of abundant harvests. They did not merit the immeasurable expansiveness of the divine bounty, but their needs were supplied on the basis of his matchless generosity, not as a reward for their unswerving devotion.'[2] Setting out on an adventurous journey through a huge inhospitable wilderness towards the Promised Land, the people needed to be reassured of God's blessing.

Peace comes to those (men and women) whose lives are marked by self-denial and self-control, such as the Nazirites (from a Hebrew word meaning 'separated' or 'consecrated') of whom we read in the verses leading up to this benediction (vv. 1–21). We cannot expect God's peace if we don't give ourselves fully to him. The disobedient and self-willed will not know his peace.

This priestly benediction reveals sparkling facets of God's gracious dealings with his people.

God's promise

The command of God to Aaron, and his sons, to pronounce this benediction is equivalent to the promise of God to bestow the blessings mentioned: preservation, pardon and peace. The prayer implies a promise. This benediction is certainly a prayer, because Aaron, the high priest, says 'The LORD bless you' (v. 24). Aaron could not bestow blessing, but the Triune God 'has blessed us in Christ with every spiritual blessing' including election, adoption, redemption and the Holy Spirit, whose presence in our hearts is a guarantee of an everlasting inheritance (Eph. 1:3–14). The gracious God 'gives generously to all' his children (James 1:5).

God's command to pronounce a benediction came to Aaron, the Jewish high priest, who offered a sacrifice for Israel on the annual Day of Atonement (Lev. 16). The priest lifted his hands, stained with blood, to bless the worshippers. God blesses us through Christ, the great high priest, who shed his blood to save us.

God's people

God does not command Aaron to bless all the nations; he only blesses the Israelites (v. 23). The church, as 'the Israel of God', now enjoys the blessings and promises of this benediction (Gal. 6:16). It is true that Jesus taught that God is kind to everyone, 'Your Father who is in heaven ...

makes his sun rise on the evil and on the good, and sends rain on the just and the unjust' (Matt. 5:45). However, he is only the Father of Christians; he is '*your* Father' (emphasis added), and therefore he has a deep love for his children and looks after them with special care. The Numbers 6 benediction belongs only to those who seek the Lord for his pardon. Do you belong to him? Is he 'your Father'?

Whom did Aaron mean when he used the word 'you' in verse 24? In English, we say 'you' when we talk to a group or when we talk to an individual. In Hebrew there is a word for addressing many and another word for speaking to someone personally. In Numbers 6:24 it is the word for talking with a person face-to-face. When Aaron pronounced the benediction on the whole nation he was also blessing each person individually. 'Surrounded by thousands of other pilgrims, individuals might feel lost in the vast crowd. With such a deliberate, repeated emphasis on the personal nature of these blessings, these travellers had no reason to doubt the concern of a loving God for each one of them.'[3] Each person is precious to God! The Lord has an intimate knowledge and a one-to-one relationship with every one of his people. The Christian can say with the apostle Paul, 'The Son of God, who loved *me* and gave himself for *me*' (Gal. 2:20, emphasis added)

God's power

God the omnipotent defender promised to protect his people when they travelled on from Sinai. 'Behold, I send an angel before you to guard you on the way and to bring you to the place that I have prepared' (Exod. 23:20).

According to the Strong's Concordance,[4] the word 'keep' in Numbers 6:24 means 'to hedge about' and brings to mind Satan's observation when considering Job (Job 1:10–11). The sovereign God allowed Satan to take some of the hedge down to test Job. Nevertheless, it was the same Sovereign who also kept this godly man during his dark affliction. This word 'kept' also anticipates the benediction of Jude 24–25: 'Now to him who is able to keep you from stumbling and to present you blameless before the presence of his glory with great joy, to the only God, our Saviour, through Jesus Christ our Lord, be glory, majesty, dominion, and authority, before all time and now and for ever. Amen.'

There are many dangers on the journey of life. Therefore we ought to pray, each day, to our heavenly Father and mighty guardian, 'And lead us not into temptation, but deliver us from evil' (Matt.6:13). Those who sincerely offer this prayer will avoid walking deliberately into situations where they are liable to be tempted.

God's pleasure

The phrase, 'make his face to shine upon you' (Num. 6:25) alludes to the sun that gives light and heat and causes the crops to grow. It means that God is the source of spiritual life and growth. The words 'The LORD lift up his countenance upon you' (v. 26) are translated in the NIV as 'the LORD turn his face towards you'. They suggest the smiles of a parent who is pleased with his children when they do well, perhaps passing an exam at school or reaching another grade while learning to play the piano. On the other hand, the parent wears a frown when the child is disobedient. Nevertheless, 'behind a frowning providence he [God] hides a smiling face', as William Cowper proved in periods of bleakest depression.[5]

Moses frequently emerged from God's presence with a shining face (Exod. 34:29–33). This benediction anticipates a time when all his people, not just Moses, will know the 'shining face' of God's approval because of the atoning death of the Lord Jesus Christ.

God's pardon

Aaron prayed for the Lord to 'be gracious' to his people (Num. 6:25). After the incident of the golden calf Moses had pleaded with God to be gracious to his people. As a result of his intercession God spared the

Israelites and proclaimed, 'The LORD [is] a God merciful and gracious, slow to anger, and abounding in steadfast love and faithfulness' (Exod.34:6).

The gracious God pardons sinners. 'Who is a God like you, pardoning iniquity and passing over transgression for the remnant of his inheritance? He does not retain his anger for ever, because he delights in steadfast love. He will again have compassion on us; he will tread our iniquities underfoot. You will cast all our sins into the depths of the sea' (Micah 7:18–19). Calvary displays God's willingness to pardon sin and forgive transgression. The holy God punished his own sinless Son in the place of his people.

God's peace

Aaron prayed, 'The LORD ... give you peace' (Num. 6:26) as he blessed the Israelites. Viewing this petition with New Testament eyes, we may discern three layers of God's peace. Firstly, the believer knows peace *with* God: 'Since we have been justified by faith, we have peace with God through our Lord Jesus Christ' (Rom. 5:1). Christ's death appeased God's wrath. He bore God's wrath instead of the sinner. God declared his Son guilty so that he might declare the believer not guilty. Secondly, the believer experiences the peace *of* God even in adverse circumstances. The apostle Paul wrote of this peace from a prison cell in Rome: 'The peace of God, which surpasses all understanding, will guard your hearts and your minds in Christ Jesus ... The God of peace will be with you' (Phil. 4:7, 9). We obtain this peace through prayer. This peace brings contentment (Phil. 4:6, 10–13). Jeremiah Burroughs, a seventeenth-century Puritan, rightly described contentment as 'a rare jewel'.[6] We are rich indeed, if we have this jewel! Thirdly, the believer desires peace with everyone. He takes to heart Paul's exhortation to the Romans, 'If possible, so far as it depends on you, live peaceably with all' (Rom. 12:18).

God's presence

What is the meaning of God's promise in Numbers 6:27, 'So shall they put my name upon the people of Israel, and I will bless them'? The phrase 'my name upon the people' means that God identifies with his people in their joys and in their sorrows. This privilege carries with it responsibility; we represent God in this world. Unbelievers judge God by our conduct. As Christians we bear Christ's name. What impression do we give of him?

This final verse in Numbers 6 is the divine Amen to Aaron's blessing: 'So shall they put my name upon the people of Israel, and I will bless them.' We ought to notice the emphatic 'I will' (v. 27); no devil in hell or wicked person on earth can stop the almighty God fulfilling his purposes. God is with his people; he becomes one with them. He promises to make good the blessing pronounced by the priests.

NOTES

1 Based on a quotation from Billy Graham: *Draper's Book of Quotations for the Christian World* (Wheaton, Illinois: Tyndale House, 1992), entry 8470 in the section on peace.

2 Raymond Brown, *The Message of Numbers—Journey to the Promised Land* (Bible Speaks Today; Leicester: Inter-Varsity Press, 2002), p.57.

3 Brown, *Numbers*, p.57.

4 James Strong, *Strong's Hebrew and Greek Dictionaries* (electronic edition, STEP Files © 2003, QuickVerse, a division of Findex.com, Inc); *The New Strong's Expanded Dictionary of Bible Words: Hebrew and Greek* (Nashville, Tennessee: Thomas Nelson, 2002).

5 William Cowper, 'God moves in a mysterious way'.

6 Jeremiah Burroughs (1599–1646), *Rare Jewel of Christian Contentment* (1648; repr. Edinburgh: Banner of Truth Trust, 1964). Grace Publications published *Learning to be happy*, a simplified abridgement, in 1988. A Kindle version of the 1648 edition is available from Amazon UK.

Ascribe greatness to God!

I will proclaim the name of the LORD; ascribe greatness to our God! (Deut. 32:3)

M oses, 120 years old, knows that he will die soon. How does he spend his final days on earth? Teaching and singing! We have his parting instructions in Deuteronomy 31 and his song in Deuteronomy 32. Following the teaching and the singing, the aged Moses blesses the twelve tribes of Israel in chapter 33. The short concluding chapter 34, added by an editor, relates Moses' death. God himself buried his servant in an unmarked grave (Deut. 34:5–7). Christian leaders die but God continues his work: Joshua followed Moses in leading God's people.

What is Moses' subject in Deuteronomy 32? I would suggest that five words at the end of verse 3 sum up this song: 'ascribe greatness to our God!' Moses closes his life with a doxology of praise to God. His song contains variations on the theme of God's greatness. To put that another way, God's greatness is like a diamond with various facets.

How do we ascribe greatness to God? The first part of verse 3 answers the question: 'I will proclaim the name of the LORD'. We proclaim his name as we adore him in worship, as we talk about him, and as we live holy lives.

The greatness of God's works and ways

Moses contrasts God's holy character with the sinful conduct of his people (vv. 4–6). God was righteous, upright and faithful; Israel was unfaithful, perverse and rebellious.

The term 'ways' in verse 4 suggests a road; the paths of each of our lives are known to God because he has planned them. God determines the place and circumstances of our birth and of our death, and all the events between birth and death. However, we are not like pieces on a chessboard that have no choice about where the players move them. God gives us the ability to make choices. We are accountable to him for our actions; this is evident from the accusations that God makes against Israel in Deuteronomy 32.

The affairs of the nations also fulfil the decrees of the sovereign King who is 'the Most High' (v. 8). This title emphasises his authority over all the nations. The phrase, 'when he divided mankind' in verse 8 recalls Genesis 11, where we read about the building of the Tower of Babel, probably a shrine to idol gods. At that time, everyone spoke one language. Listen to the proud builders: 'Come, let us build ourselves a city and a tower with its top in the heavens, and let us make a name for ourselves, lest we be dispersed over the face of the whole earth' (Gen. 11:4). Building the tower was rebellion against God. How does he react? He asserts his sovereignty. He confuses their language and scatters the human race to different parts of the earth (Gen. 11:5–9).

At the end of Deuteronomy 32:8, we read that God 'fixed the borders of the peoples according to the number of the sons of God [Israel]'. John MacArthur explains these words: 'God ordained a plan where the number of nations (70 according to Gen. 10) corresponded to the number of the children of Israel (70 according to Gen. 46:27). Further, as God gave the nations their lands, He established their boundaries, leaving enough land to sustain their expected population.'[1]

The greatness of God the Rock

Five times in this song, Moses describes God as a rock. The first reference is in verse 4: 'The Rock, his work is perfect, for all his ways are justice.' Whether we look at his work in creation, salvation or providence, he does everything perfectly. All that he does enhances his glory and gives us cause to ascribe greatness to him.

After each day of creation, 'God saw that it was good' (Gen. 1:10, 12, 18, 21, 25) and on the final day, 'God saw everything that he had made, and behold, it was very good' (Gen. 1:31). Adam and Eve's sin spoilt God's perfect world (Gen. 3). Nevertheless, God had already included human sin in his wise decrees and had already designed a perfect redemption through the death of his Son (Rom. 8:28–32; Eph. 1:3–10; 1 Peter 1:18–21).

God cares for his people: we call this providence. Here too, God's works are perfect. He works everything, even the bad events, for his glory and the good of his children (Rom.8:28). We see an example of this in the life of Joseph. After the death of his father Jacob, Joseph reassured his brothers, who had sold him into slavery, with this truth: 'You meant evil against me, but God meant it for good' (Gen.50:20).

Moses not only celebrates God's perfect works, but also praises him for his justice. 'All his ways are justice. A God of faithfulness and without iniquity, just and upright is he' (Deut. 32:4). He always treats us fairly. He will never deceive us nor desert us. He will defend us and protect us from Satan's accusations. He will love us for ever (Rom. 8:31–39).

The second mention of the Rock is in verse 15: 'Jeshurun grew fat, and kicked; ... then he forsook God who made him and scoffed at the Rock of his salvation.' We read a similar lament in verse 18: 'You were unmindful of the Rock that bore you, and you forgot the God who gave you birth.' 'Jeshurun' (see also 33:5, 26; Isa. 44:2) comes from a word that means 'upright'—the 'upright' nation bent over with sinful conduct.

Israel had rejected God, her mighty creator and bountiful provider; she acted like an ungrateful child towards her divine Father (vv. 5–6) and behaved like an animal kicking against its kind master (v. 15). God their Rock had delivered them from Egyptian bondage. He brought them through the Red Sea to freedom. In the wilderness he had provided food lavishly for forty years (vv. 13–14). Now they stood on the verge of a land 'flowing with milk and honey', the land promised to them from the days of the patriarch Abraham (Gen. 12:7; 13:14–18; 17:8).

Why had Israel abandoned God? Because they had worshipped images, 'They stirred him to jealousy with strange gods; with abominations they provoked him to anger. They sacrificed to demons that were no gods, to gods, they had never known, to new gods that had come recently, whom your fathers had never dreaded' (vv. 16–17).

God, like a husband whose wife had abandoned him for another lover, felt jealous and angry. God reacted to this rejection by hiding his face of favour from them (vv. 19–20). Israel's idolatry eventually led to exile in Babylon (v. 21). The nation's sin often brought military defeat (see for example, vv. 30–31). God her Rock had permitted defeats but not destruction; he still loved and protected his undeserving people. God always takes seriously the sins of his people (compare 1 Peter 4:17–18).

Do we sometimes, like Israel, take for granted his salvation and his kindness to us? Do we sometimes abandon him for the 'gods' of popularity, possessions and pleasures? False gods—then and now—fail their devotees; only God the Rock is dependable (vv. 37–38). This is something for which to ascribe greatness to our God! Matthew Henry comments: 'Those who trust to any rock but God will find it sand in the day of their distress; it will fail them when they need it most.'[2]

The greatness of God's love

Another aspect of God's greatness is his unchanging love for his people even though they had rebelled against him. It was God who chose Israel (vv. 9, 18), not because they deserved his favour but because of his grace (Deut. 7:6–10). The chosen race are, 'therefore [to] be careful to do the commandments and the statutes and the rules that I command you' says God (Deut. 7:11). Grace demands obedience!

From all the races of the earth God chose Israel and gave them the land of Canaan. He instructed Moses how to divide this land between the twelve tribes that grew out of the family of Jacob. Each tribe had a portion or an inheritance. God spoke of the Jewish race as 'Jacob his allotted heritage' (Deut. 32:9). Heritage speaks of an invaluable privilege, but the name Jacob indicates the Lord's unmerited love. Jacob's name, which means 'supplanter' or 'deceiver', accurately described his character. Nevertheless, God loved sinful Jacob. God's eternal plan was that from this race, which grew from the descendants of Abraham, Isaac and Jacob, would emerge the Messiah, Jesus the Saviour of the world. He would die to save sinners like Jacob.

Moses highlights God's love in verses 10–12. We read that 'He [God] found him [Israel]' (v.10). We, like Israel, were lost, like helpless and hopeless sheep 'in a desert land and in the howling waste of the wilderness' (v. 10) until the divine Shepherd found us. We had no desire or ability to find him.

The gracious God encircles us with his tender care. We are 'kept ... as the apple of his eye' (v. 10). Believers are 'at the core and heart of God's vision—his care for his people cannot be missed'.[3] This 'apple of his eye' metaphor also means that just as poking the eye causes pain, so those who hurt God's people offend God. It is like poking God in the eye! He feels for us when we suffer: 'In all their affliction he was afflicted, and the angel of his presence saved them; in his love and in his pity he redeemed them; he lifted them up and carried them all the days of old' (Isa.63:9; see also Heb. 2:17–18; 4:14–16). It was God alone who guided and cared for his people (Deut. 32:12).

Verse 10 finds an echo in Psalm 17:8: 'Keep me as the apple of your eye; hide me in the shadow of your wings.' Philip Eveson makes an interesting comment on this verse: 'As God kept Israel as "the apple of his eye" so David pleads that God would keep him. The tender Hebrew idiom (literally, "as the little one, daughter of an eye") probably refers to the tiny image of the little one in the pupil of the mother's eye as she looks down on the baby at her breast. Further, as God protected Israel like an eagle with its wings outspread so David asks that he would find a hiding place "under the shadow of your wings" from the wicked enemies who surround him and are after his life.'[4]

Moses compares God to an eagle that nurtures and protects its young in the nest. The eagle flutters over its brood to encourage them to fly and is ready to catch any that are in difficulties or that are not yet strong enough to fly (v. 11). Believers find security in the arms of God. 'The eternal God is your dwelling place, and underneath are the everlasting arms' (Deut. 33:27). The phrase—'bearing them'—the eagle bearing its young—anticipates Isaiah 40:11: 'He [Christ] will tend his flock like a shepherd; he will gather the lambs in his arms; he will carry them in his bosom, and gently lead those that are with young.' How should we respond to God's matchless love and ceaseless care? We ought to 'ascribe greatness to our God'!

The word 'flutters' (translated as 'hovers' in the NIV) recalls Genesis 1:2: 'The earth was without form and void, and darkness was over the face of the deep. And the Spirit of God [The Holy Spirit] was hovering over the face of the waters.' God's Spirit hovers over believers, whom Paul calls 'a new creation' (2 Cor. 5:17). In the previous chapter, the apostle wrote, 'For God, who said, "Let light shine out of darkness", has shone in our hearts to give the light of the knowledge of the glory of God in the face of Jesus Christ' (2 Cor. 4:6).

NOTES

1   John MacArthur, *The MacArthur Study Bible NKJV* (Dallas: Word Publishing, 1997), p.297 (note on Deuteronomy 32:8).

2   Matthew Henry's comments on Deuteronomy 32:26. I have the digital version produced by Parsons Church Group, a division of Findex.com, Omaha, Nebraska, USA. Hendrickson Publishers, Massachusetts, USA published in 2008 a hardback, complete and unabridged, edition. A Kindle version is available from Amazon UK.

3   John Currid, *Deuteronomy* (EP Study Commentary; Darlington: Evangelical Press, 2006), p499.

4   Philip Eveson, *Psalms*, vol. 1 (Welwyn Commentary; Darlington: Evangelical Press, 2014), p.112.

A godly mother's praise

My heart exults in the LORD. (1 Sam. 2:1)

'Hannah, why do you weep … Am I not more to you than ten sons?' Elkanah asks his childless wife. We ought not to misjudge Elkanah because of his question (1 Sam. 1:8). We read that he gave double portions of the sacrificial meat to Hannah 'because he loved her, though the LORD had closed her womb' (1 Sam. 1:5). Children are a gift from God (Ps. 127:3–5). Conception is a blessing from God; however, infertility is not a punishment from God—though that was the normal Jewish assumption regarding childless women.

Elkanah, who was rich enough to afford two wives, was in breach of God's blueprint for marriage: one man and one wife (Gen. 2:24–25). Peninnah, the child-bearing wife, derides Hannah because of her barrenness, especially at the time of the annual visit to God's house (1 Sam. 1:1–2, 6). The word 'provoke' means 'to thunder against' and reads as 'thunder' in 1 Samuel 2:10. However, not only should we commend Hannah for patiently bearing with Peninnah's derision, but perhaps we should also not be too critical of Elkanah because of his domestic situation. He did not have the full light of God's revelation that we have. Maybe, because of Hannah's barrenness, he took a second wife to raise a family. To his credit, he went every year 'to worship and to sacrifice to the LORD of hosts at Shiloh' (1 Sam. 1:3).

Elkanah and his family lived about 1100 BC in Ramathaim-zophim, Ephraim (later known as Arimathea, Matt. 27:57) at the time when the judges were about to be replaced by the monarchy. Gordon Keddie comments: 'And so, although the people involved were quite unaware of it at the time, the initial step towards the establishment of David's royal throne was the childlessness of a Levite's wife!' [Hannah]. A few pages later he writes: 'Samuel would be a link in the chain of salvation' because he anointed David the ancestor of Christ.[1]

Pain

Hannah in her deep distress 'prayed to the LORD and wept bitterly' (1 Sam. 1:10), and 'continued praying' (v. 12), as she 'was speaking in her heart' (v. 13). Her sorrow was bitter, though she was not bitter against God. Rather she was simply 'pouring out [her] soul before the LORD' because she was full of 'great anxiety and vexation' (vv. 15–16). Eli, elderly, overweight and very short-sighted (1 Sam. 4:14–18), sees a woman with moving lips, and presumably a shaking body, but he cannot hear her words or discern the reason for her unusual behaviour, so he wrongly accuses her of being drunk (vv. 12–15). Are we too quick to criticize or become impatient with those who are sad because we don't fully understand the cause of their pain? Like Eli we may jump to the wrong conclusions, and consequently cause more sorrow.

Prayer

What does Hannah do in her anguish? She 'prayed to the LORD' (Jehovah/Yahweh) (v.10) who delivered his people from Egyptian bondage (Exod. 14). He is also called 'the LORD of hosts' (1 Sam. 1:3, 11), the mighty God who created the stars (Isa. 40:26), commands a vast army of angels (Ps. 103:20–21) and leads the armies of Israel (Ex. 12:41; Ps. 46:7, 11). This title, first used in 1 Samuel 1:3, occurs nearly 300 times in God's Word. He was well able to answer this sorrowful woman's prayer.

As Hannah prayed, did she recall God's kindness to barren Sarah (Gen. 11:30) and to Rachel (Gen. 29:31; 30:22–23)? God who gave Sarah and Rachel children could surely give infertile Hannah a son. When distressed we, like Hannah, should earnestly seek the help of 'the Father of mercies and God of all comfort' (2 Cor. 1:3). He does not misconstrue our emotions. He feels for us! God uses the jibes of Peninnah to cause Hannah to pray. We ought to thank God for trials if they send us to his throne!

Why did God permit Hannah's inability to conceive? Let's broaden that question: Why does the gracious God, who loves us much more than Elkanah loved Hannah, allow us to suffer? Dale Ralph Davis wisely remarks, 'When his people are without strength, without resources, without hope, without human gimmicks—then he loves to stretch forth his hand from heaven. Once we see where God often begins we will understand how we may be encouraged.'[2]

Weeping Hannah makes a vow to God. 'O LORD of hosts, if you will indeed look on the affliction of your servant and remember me and not forget your servant, but will give to your servant a son, then I will give him to the LORD all the days of his life, and no razor shall touch his head' (1 Sam. 1:11). The uncut hair expresses Hannah's consecration of Samuel to the Nazirite vow (Num. 6:1–21), just as Manoah's wife dedicated Samson to God (Judg. 13). She is not trying to bribe or bargain with God; her prayer is rather an indication of her whole-hearted devotion to God. She comes humbly as a 'servant' (used three times), deserving nothing, but appeals to the gracious God to turn her sorrow into joy. As a servant she submits herself to God's sovereign will.

In response to Hannah's request, 'remember me' (1 Sam. 1:11), we read that 'the LORD remembered' desolate Hannah (v. 19). She was much on God's mind. He makes a promise through Eli, after he had properly perceived the situation. 'Go in peace', he says, 'and the God of Israel grant your petition that you have made to him'—this is the priest's special benediction for a devout woman (v. 17). It is the only incident in Scripture of a priest blessing an individual. She replies, 'Let your servant find favour in your eyes.' Confident that God had answered her prayer she eats food with a cheerful face (v. 18).

Because God remembered Hannah, 'in due time [she] conceived and bore a son, and she called his name Samuel, for she said, "I have asked for him from the LORD"' (vv. 19–20). Scholars debate the meaning of the name Samuel; but it most likely means 'heard of God'. Praise replaces her pain. The Lord kept his promise; did Hannah fulfil hers? Yes she did! When she had weaned the child, probably about the age of three, she took her precious son to Shiloh. Listen to her words on this occasion, '"For this child I prayed, and the LORD has granted my petition that I made to him. Therefore I have lent him to the LORD. As long as he lives, he is lent [given] to the LORD"' (vv. 27–28). Elkanah could have overruled his wife if he disagreed with her vow (Num. 30:6–15), but it is clear from verse 23 that he too was willing to offer his son as a living sacrifice to the Lord.

Commentators differ about the interpretation of the final words of verse 28, 'And he worshipped the LORD there'—is this a reference to Elkanah or to Samuel? The NKJV translates 'he' as 'they', which could then refer to Eli and Samuel, or even to both Elkanah and Hannah, who worshipped God when they left young Samuel at Shiloh.

Hannah was a remarkable woman who gave birth to a remarkable son. The boy served God by serving the priest (1 Sam. 2:11). It is apparent that he followed in the footsteps of his pious mother because his love and obedience to God stand in contrast to the wickedness of Eli's sons, Hophni and Phinehas (1 Sam. 2:12–26). God rejects them, but shows favour to Samuel (1 Sam. 2:26). As the first of the prophets he called God's people to forsake their idols so as to worship God alone.

What happened to Hannah? The good God rewarded her costly obedience, 'Indeed the LORD visited Hannah, and she conceived and bore three sons and two daughters. And the boy Samuel grew in the presence of the LORD' (1 Sam. 2:21).

Praise

How could Hannah, the tender mother, leave Samuel, her darling son, with Eli, the aged priest? We would expect floods of tears! However, her focus is not on Samuel but on God; she 'exults in the LORD', who gave her strength to devote her son to him (2 Sam. 2:1). She looks beyond the gift to the Giver in a canticle of praise. Hannah rejoices in God her Saviour, who delivered her from her childlessness through the birth of her son. God rescues us from sin through the gift of his only Son (John 3:16; 2 Cor. 9:15).

Hannah's psalm of praise has striking similarities to David's song (2 Sam. 22:2–51), and its themes are picked up by Mary in what is known as the Magnificat (Luke 1:46–55). Hannah praises God as the one who is holy, all-powerful, all-knowing, just and sovereign (1 Sam. 2:2–8), and in so doing she looks forward to the coming Messiah-Saviour (vv. 9–10).

GOD IS HOLY

'There is none holy like the LORD; there is none besides you' (v. 2). Moses, in the presence of the holy God at Horeb, 'hid his face, for he was afraid to look at God' (Exod. 3:6). Isaiah felt overwhelmed by his sinfulness when he heard seraphim proclaiming God's holiness: 'One [of the seraphim] called to another and said: "Holy, holy, holy is the LORD of hosts; the whole earth is full of his glory" … And I said: "Woe is me! For I am lost; for I am a man of unclean lips"' (Isa. 6:1–4). Nevertheless, the holy God lives in the humble: 'Thus says the One who is high and lifted up, who inhabits eternity, whose name is Holy: "I dwell in the high and lofty place and also with him who is of a contrite and lowly spirit"' (Isa. 57:15). He alone is God, and he alone is absolutely holy. We can approach the holy God through Christ!

GOD IS ALL-POWERFUL

'There is no rock like our God' (1 Sam. 2:2). At the end of his life Moses sang about God the Rock, 'For their rock is not as our Rock' (Deut. 32:31). As we have seen in chapter 5, the Rock motif occurs several times in Moses' final song. Paul identifies the Rock as Christ who was with his nomad people in the wilderness (I Cor. 10:1–5). The Rock did not fail sorrowing Hannah. He is our Rock in the storms of life (Matt. 7:24–27).

GOD IS ALL-KNOWING

'Talk no more so very proudly, let not arrogance come from your mouth; for the LORD is a God of knowledge' (1 Sam. 2:3). God heard Peninnah's cruel provocation; he saw Hannah's tears. Our tears are precious to him (see Ps. 56:8).

GOD IS JUST

'By him actions are weighed' (1 Sam. 2:3). The classic example of this is when Belshazzar, King of Babylon, saw the handwriting on the wall telling him, 'you have been weighed in the balances and found wanting' (Dan. 5:27). Everyone (2 Cor. 5:10) will give an account to the God who sees all things (Heb. 4:12–13).

GOD IS SOVEREIGN

One way in which we see the sovereignty of God revealed is the way he reverses circumstances. He breaks down the proud (such as Peninnah) and lifts up those who are poor and vulnerable (such as Hannah) (1 Sam. 2:4). It is God who gives children but childlessness is not a punishment (v. 5; 1 Sam. 1:5). The number 'seven' in verse 5 is the number of completion; it indicates God's blessing. The sovereign God, who is the creator and sustainer of the world (v. 8), determines when we are born and when we die (v. 6), and whether we are rich or poor (vv. 5a, 7). He 'raises up the poor from dust' (v. 8) means that whatever we achieve in life is due to God's goodness and grace. Verse 8 is a good description of what God does for us spiritually—he turns beggars into princes! Furthermore, he protects the faithful (v. 9) and destroys the wicked (vv. 9–10). Verse 9a finds an echo in the doxology of Jude 24–25: 'Now to him who is able to keep you from stumbling and to present you blameless before the presence of his glory with great joy, to the only God, our

Saviour, through Jesus Christ our Lord, be glory, majesty, dominion, and authority, before all time and now and for ever. Amen.'

Promise

The key to understanding verse 10 is the promise, 'The LORD ... will give strength to his king and exalt the horn [power] of his anointed.' Who is God's anointed? Ethan, the psalmist wrote, 'I have found David, my servant; with my holy oil I have anointed him, so that my hand shall be established with him; my arm also shall strengthen him' (Ps. 89:20–21).[3] However, David, Israel's second king, had died many years before this psalm. So who is the anointed? He is the one whose 'offspring shall endure for ever, his throne as long as the sun before me. Like the moon it shall be established for ever, a faithful witness in the skies' (Ps. 89:36–37). There can be no doubt that the anointed is a greater than David, the Lord Jesus Christ, the everlasting king, whose throne is for ever (Heb. 1:8). He is the Lord's Anointed of whom we read in Psalm 2. The title Messiah (Hebrew) and Christ (Greek) means 'anointed'. God the Holy Spirit anointed God the Son at his baptism (Matt. 3:13–17). Like David he was the Shepherd-King. God has kept his word—Jesus Christ has come!

Comfort

Hannah is an example of how God 'heals the broken-hearted and binds up their wounds' (Ps. 147:3). So is John Calvin, who after the death of his wife Idelette wrote, 'May the Lord Jesus ... support me under this heavy affliction, which would certainly have overcome me, had not He, who raises up the prostrate, strengthens the weak, and refreshes the weary, stretched forth His hand from heaven to me.'[4]

Chapter 6

NOTES

1 Gordon J Keddie, *Dawn of a Kingdom* (Welwyn Commentary; Welwyn: Evangelical Press, 1988), pp.18, 22.

2 Dale Ralph Davis, *1 Samuel: Looking on the heart* (Fearn, Ross-shire: Christian Focus, 2000), p.13.

3 See chapter 13.

4 Davis, *1 Samuel*, p.19.

A wise king's benediction

Solomon … stood and blessed all the assembly of Israel with a loud voice saying. 'Blessed be the LORD who has given rest to his people Israel, according to all that he promised.' (1 Kings 8:54–61)

It was a day never forgotten; many would look back and see it as the great highlight of their lives. We read about this memorable day in 1 Kings 8. The people witnessed the dedication of Solomon's temple in Jerusalem, which had taken seven years to build. We read about the preparation and construction of the temple in chapters 5–7 (see also 2 Chr. 2–4). The building began 480 years after God delivered Israel from bondage in Egypt and in the fourth year of king Solomon's reign; he ascended the throne in 972 BC (1 Kings 6:1, 37).

What events occurred on this memorable dedication day?

First, the moving of the ark and the tent of meeting (vv. 1–13; 2 Chr. 5). 'The tent of meeting' was a temporary place for worship in Gibeon. The Ark of the Covenant was the symbol of God's presence, now brought back from the house of Obed-Edom (2 Sam. 6:1–15). The priests placed the Ark behind the thick veil in the Most Holy Place. The high priest sprinkled blood on the gold-covered lid, the mercy seat, on the annual Day of Atonement (Lev. 16).

Second, Solomon blesses the Lord (vv. 12–21; 2 Chr. 6:1–11).

Third, Solomon's prayer of dedication (vv.22–53; 2 Chr. 6:12–42). We read in 2 Chronicles.7:1–3 that fire came from heaven to consume the sacrifices after Solomon's prayer. The people fall on their faces to worship God.

Fourth, Solomon blesses the people (vv. 54–61).

Fifth, Solomon's feast (vv. 62–66; 2 Chr. 7:4–10).

The builders completed the temple eleven months before these celebrations. Why then had Solomon delayed so long? The clue is found in verse 2. It would appear that he wanted the dedication day to coincide with 'the feast in the month Ethanim, which is the seventh month.' The seventh month, later known as Tishri, was equivalent to our September/October. The feast was the Feast of the Tabernacles (also called the Feast of Booths or the Feast of Ingathering). This last of the three yearly festivals[1] was not only a harvest feast, but also a commemoration of the time when Israel's forefathers moved into permanent houses in the land of Canaan after years of living in temporary booths (tents) in the wilderness (Lev. 23:33–44; Deut. 16:13–15). The Feast of Tabernacles was also significant because God had demanded that the people of Israel renew their covenant with him every seven years during this feast (Deut. 31:10–11). The dedication of Solomon's temple was a time for the nation to rededicate themselves to their God.

Who would ever forget what happened once the ark was in the temple? 'And when the priests came out of the Holy Place, a cloud filled the house of the LORD, so that the priests could not stand to minister because of the cloud, for the glory of the LORD filled the house of the LORD' (vv. 10–11). This cloud was seen at Mount Sinai after the people of Israel were miraculously delivered from their bondage in Egypt (Exod. 24:15–17), and it appeared again when the tabernacle was completed (Exod. 40:34–38; Num. 9:15–23). God guided his people by the cloud in the day and protected them by a pillar of fire at night (Exod. 13:21–22; 14:19–20). The cloud was the sign that God was moving into his house.

Dale Ralph Davis explains the significance of this cloud: 'The cloud is visible and so is a sign of God's presence, yet the cloud also conceals—they do not see Yahweh in the full blaze of his presence … The cloud both is Yahweh's glory and covers Yahweh's glory; it both reveals and conceals. The cloud and thick darkness signify that there is a certain *hiddenness* about God; there is much we cannot see and do not know.'[2]

The invisible God became visible in Christ (Col. 1:15; Heb. 1:3). We will see his face! (Rev. 22:4; 1 John 3:2).

Gold was a major feature of Solomon's temple, mentioned ten times in 1 Kings 6:20–35. Why so much gold? Here is Dale Ralph Davis again: 'I suggest that the splendour of the temple is meant to reflect the splendour of Israel's God, that the temple's gold points to Yahweh's glory.'[3]

Near the altar

When Solomon prayed, and then blessed the people, he was 'before the altar of the LORD' (1 Kings 8:22, 54)—the place of atonement. Solomon offered sacrifices when the ark came to Jerusalem (vv. 4–6). The unblemished animals died instead of the guilty offenders to conciliate the holy God. After the prayer and benediction Solomon offered more sacrifices to God (vv. 62–64). It is clear from the book of Hebrews that these sacrifices could never take away sin. They pointed forward to Christ, who 'offered for all time a single sacrifice for sins'. We approach God with confidence 'by the blood of Jesus' (Heb. 10:4, 11–12, 19).

We read that when Solomon prayed he 'spread out his hands towards heaven' (1 Kings 8:22) and 'knelt with hands outstretched towards heaven' (v. 54), indicative of his dependence on God. Several times he described himself as God's servant (vv. 24–26, 29–30) and God's people as 'your servants' (v. 32). A recurring phrase (with variations) was, 'Listen in heaven your dwelling place, and when you hear, forgive' (v. 30). The sinful king comes humbly before the holy and almighty sovereign.

'Blessed be the LORD'

Solomon begins his speech and his benediction with the words: 'Blessed be the LORD' (vv. 15, 56). 'This tells us that he was occupied with the Lord and what he had done. Solomon could have brought attention to himself. He could have ordered the day's events in such a way that the people praised him for his careful planning, shrewd negotiating and wise leadership. Or he could have heaped praise upon the people for all they had done to make the temple a reality. But Solomon knew the truth of the matter. The praise belonged to the Lord alone. All that he and the people had done was the result of the Lord's graciously working in them and enabling them.'[4]

Solomon's concern is God's glory, as is also evident when he told Hiram, king of Tyre: 'I intend to build a house for the name of the LORD' (1 Kings 5:5). It is instructive to place this statement alongside 2 Chronicles 2:5–6, where we read: 'The house that I am to build will be great, for our God is greater than all gods. But who is able to build him a house, since heaven, even highest heaven, cannot contain him? Who am I to build a house for him, except as a place to make offerings before him?' Solomon the king felt unworthy as he prayed to God the glorious and infinite King!

Pause to think for a moment about the fact that 'the highest heaven cannot contain you' (v. 27). 'Here he [Solomon] confesses the uncontainability, the unboxability of God. Here is the God who bursts all our categories and frustrates all our attempts to surround his majesty. Here is the immensity of God. Will God really dwell upon earth, let alone in a temple? Why, the heavens, even the highest heavens, cannot contain him! The words drip with our happy failure to get a grip on the massive majesty of God.'[5] This awesome God answered Solomon's prayer—he hears ours too (vv. 28–30; 1 Kings 9:3)!

God gives rest

Solomon blesses God 'who has given rest to his people' (v. 56). The Hebrew word translated as 'rest' describes a time of peace after war. Solomon is called a 'man of rest' (1 Chr. 22:9) because there were no wars during his reign.

This term 'rest' recalls Solomon's words in 1 Kings 5:1–5, and also helps us to understand why David could not build the temple. Solomon reminds Hiram (who supplied cedar and cypress timber),

you know that David my father could not build a house for the name of the LORD his God because of the warfare with which his enemies surrounded him, until the LORD put them under the soles of his feet. But now the LORD my God has given me rest on every side. There is neither adversary nor misfortune. And so I intend to build the house for the name of the LORD my God, as the LORD said to David my father, 'Your son, whom I will set on your throne in your place, shall build a house for my name.'

David paved the way for Solomon to build the temple by defeating his enemies. Roger Ellsworth comments:

Great domestic projects cannot be undertaken and successfully completed when a nation is engaged in warfare. War syphons time and resources away from other concerns. Solomon was under no illusions about how his kingdom had come to enjoy the peace that made it possible to build the temple. It was not just a fortunate turn of circumstances. It was rather because, as he stated, the Lord had given him rest.[6]

Now that God had given his people rest, it was time to build him a temple—a resting-place.

The church on earth is the 'church militant' fighting indwelling sin, resisting the ensnaring influence of unbelievers and standing against Satan. God gives us armour to fight in his army (Eph. 6:10–20). God gives to the 'church triumphant' in heaven rest from spiritual warfare. At Calvary Christ conquered Satan (Col. 2:15) and, therefore, when he returns he will throw the devil into the everlasting 'lake of fire' (Rev. 20:10–15). This will also be the destination of all who reject the Lord Jesus Christ. Jesus spoke alarming words to rebellious people, whom he compared to goats: 'Depart from me, you cursed, into the eternal fire prepared for the devil and his angels' (Matt. 25:41). Had they committed some vile sins, such as murder or the abuse of children? No! They had not cared for God's needy people; to show compassion was to serve Christ (Matt. 25:42–45). He welcomes the sheep, Christians, to 'inherit the kingdom prepared ... from the foundation of the world' (Matt. 25:34). Both heaven and hell are never-ending: 'These will go away into eternal punishment, but the righteous into eternal life' (Matt. 25:46). The ungodly will have no rest in hell, a place of torment; whereas, the godly in heaven are blessed and 'rest from their labours' (Rev. 14:9–13).

It is only those who respond to the Saviour's gracious invitation in Matthew 11:28 who will enter the everlasting rest of heaven—a theme developed in Hebrews chapters 3 and 4. Jesus said: 'Come to me; all who labour and are heavy laden, and I will give you rest.' Trying to achieve salvation by our own futile efforts leaves us 'weary and burdened' (NIV). We have to stop resting on our good deeds and rest on Christ alone for salvation. Christ gives rest to those who willingly learn from him and joyfully serve him (Matt. 11:29–30).

God keeps his promises

In his benediction Solomon reminds Israel that God 'has given rest ... according to all that he promised. Not one word has failed of all his good promise' (1 Kings 8:56). These words echo Solomon's affirmation that 'the LORD, the God of Israel ... has fulfilled what he promised with his mouth to David my father' (v. 15). God had promised that Solomon would inherit his father's throne and build a temple (vv. 12–21; vv. 24–25). God kept *every* promise: 'Not one word has failed' (v. 56). 'Solomon celebrated, not a God who is generally faithful, but rather one who is perfectly faithful.'[7] God's promise drove Solomon's project. God keeping his promises is a theme that runs throughout the Bible.

God commands obedience

Solomon desires that God who has blessed Israel in the past will be with them in the future. We read in verse 57: 'The LORD our God be with us, as he was with our fathers. May he not leave us or forsake us.' Those who sincerely long for God's presence will obey him: 'Our God be with us ... that he may incline our hearts to him, to walk in all his ways and to keep his commandments ...' (vv. 57–58; 1 Kings 6:11–13).

Believers are responsible 'to walk in all his ways and to keep his commandments'; we must do the walking and the keeping (vv. 58, 61). God commands total obedience: 'all his ways' (v. 58), and expects wholehearted devotion: 'Let your heart therefore be wholly true to the LORD our God' (v. 61). Yet we are incapable of obeying if God forsakes us and if he does not 'incline our hearts to him' (v. 58). We diligently obey God as a result of him working in us. The apostle Paul makes the same point in his letter to the Philippians: 'Work out your own salvation with fear and trembling, for it is God who works in you, both to will and to work for his good pleasure' (Phil. 2:12–13). The apostle is not teaching that we can work for or towards our salvation but we are to 'work out' the salvation which we already possess. We show by our godly lives that we are genuine Christians.

It is a sad fact that wise Solomon, after urging the people to remain loyal to God, became an old fool, and that Israel, following his example, turned to idols rather than offering their worship to God alone (1 Kings 11:1–8). This unfaithfulness to the faithful God led to the divided kingdom (930 BC); the northern kingdom of Israel being defeated by the Assyrians (722 BC) and the southern kingdom of Judah being conquered by the Babylonians (586 BC). The faithful God promised to bring his people back to the land of Israel. Ezra and Nehemiah relate how God kept that promise.

Why should the people of Israel (v. 59) obey God? So that 'all the peoples of the earth may know that the LORD is God; there is no other' (v. 60). The nation of Israel was the Lord's witness in a wicked world which worshipped a multiplicity of idols (Isa. 43:10–11). Likewise, the church, which is his 'chosen race, a royal priesthood, a holy nation, a people for his own possession' is to proclaim the excellences of him who called them 'out of darkness into his marvellous light' (1 Peter 2:9).

'All the peoples of the earth may know that the LORD is God' (v. 60) anticipates the new earth when God will fulfil the promise of Isaiah 11:9: 'For the earth shall be full of the knowledge of the LORD as the waters cover the sea.' Habakkuk adds: '... filled with the knowledge of the glory of the LORD' (Hab. 2:14).

Until that day we have God's promise that he will never leave us nor forsake us (v. 57). God was with Abraham, Isaac (Gen. 26:3, 24); Jacob (Gen. 28:15; 31:3; 46:1–4); Moses (Exod. 3:12; 33:14), Joshua (Deut. 31:6–8; Josh. 1:5, 9; 3:7), and Gideon (Judg. 6:15–16). Samuel repeated this promise to the nation of Israel (1 Sam. 12:22). David encouraged Solomon with this promise to encourage him to build the temple (1 Chr. 28:20). God repeats the promise through Isaiah and Jeremiah (Isa. 41:10, 17; 43:5; 49:14–16; Jer. 1:8, 19; 20:11). Just before his ascension Christ reassured his disciples of his presence (Matt. 28:19–20). We too can claim this precious promise (Heb. 13:5).

Abundance

Solomon follows his prayer and benediction with sacrifices lasting seven days and on the eighth day, 'he sent the people away, and they blessed the king and went to their homes joyful and glad of heart for all the goodness that the LORD had shown to David his servant and to Israel his people' (vv. 65–66).

'Abundance' is the word that springs to mind when we read verses 62–64. Abundant sacrifices for the good God who is lavish in his grace! 'How great is the love the Father has lavished on us, that we should be called children of God!' (1 John 3:1, NIV). The worshippers were exuberant in their joy because the good God had kept the promises that he made to David (2 Sam. 7:12–16). In turn their king, Solomon, had proven to be a wise administrator, and they now had a beautiful temple. We ought to praise God who always keeps his promises, that he is the all-wise God who lives in the church which is his temple (Eph. 2:18–22). Paul depicts the temple as the bride that will reflect for eternity the glory of Christ the divine bridegroom (Eph. 5:25–27).

Chapter 7

NOTES

1   The three Jewish annual festivals were the Passover, the Feast of Weeks (Pentecost/harvest) and the Feast of Tabernacles. God commanded every able-bodied man to attend (Deut. 16:16).

2   Dale Ralph Davis, *The Wisdom and the Folly—An exposition of the Book of First Kings* (Fearn, Ross-Shire: Christian Focus, 2002), p.81.

3   Davis, *The Wisdom and the Folly*, p.64.

4   Roger Ellsworth, *From Glory to Ruin* (Welwyn Commentary; Darlington: Evangelical Press, 2000), p.77.

5   Davis, *The Wisdom and the Folly*, p.86.

6   Ellsworth, *From Glory to Ruin*, p.54.

7   Ellsworth, *From Glory to Ruin*, p.79.

An old king's praise and prayer

David said: 'Blessed are you, O LORD, the God of Israel our father, for ever and ever. Yours, O LORD, is the greatness and the power and the glory and the victory and the majesty, for all that is in the heavens and in the earth is yours. Yours is the kingdom, O LORD, and you are exalted as head above all …' Then David said to all the assembly, 'Bless the LORD your God.' And all the assembly blessed the LORD … and bowed their heads and paid homage to the LORD and to the king. (1 Chr. 29:10–11, 20)

Perhaps you are not a frequent reader of the first book of Chronicles, but somehow the prayer 'Yours, O LORD, is the greatness and the power and the glory and the victory and the majesty … Yours is the kingdom, O LORD' sound familiar. Why is this? Because the final doxology of what we call 'The Lord's Prayer', as said in churches of all denominations, is similar to David's prayer (Matt. 6:13). However, the words, 'For thine is the kingdom, and the power, and the glory, for ever', though found in the King James Bible Version (the Authorised Version) are missing in most other translations or confined to a footnote or inserted in italics or brackets. Did Jesus teach his disciples these words? Nineteenth-century Hebrew scholar David Brown comments: 'On a review of the evidence, the strong probability, we think, is that it was no part of the original text.'[1] Whatever view we take about the inclusion or omission of the doxology in Jesus' pattern prayer, these words are part of God's Word, as they appear in David's prayer, declaring the pre-eminence of God.

Chapter 8

David's desire

A project dear to David's heart was to build a temple—a house for the Ark of the Covenant, the symbol of God's presence[2]—in the capital city of Jerusalem. But God said to David: 'You may not build a house for my name, for you are a man of war and have shed blood ... It is Solomon your son who shall build my house ... I have chosen him to be my son, and I will be his father'. However, God's blessing depended on Solomon's obedience: 'I will establish his kingdom for ever if he continues strong in keeping my commandments and my rules, as he is today' (1 Chr. 28:1–8). David reiterates God's demand for obedience, 'Solomon , my son, know the God of your father and serve him with a whole heart and with a willing mind, for the LORD searches all hearts and understands every plan and thought. If you seek him, he will be found by you, but if you forsake him, he will cast you off for ever. Be careful now, for the LORD has chosen you to build a house for the sanctuary; be strong and do it' (vv.9–10). Tragically the wise young man became an old fool.[3]

God, who demanded obedience from Solomon, has more reason to expect those who live after Christ's life and death to live holy lives (1 Peter 1:14–21). Godly living expresses our gratitude to God for salvation.

David gave detailed instructions to the Levites (1 Chr. 23), the priests (chapter 24), the musicians (chapter 25), the gatekeepers, treasurers and other officials (chapter 26), the military and tribal leaders (chapter 27) before giving his charge to Israel and Solomon (chapter 28). Everything was completed according to God's plan (1 Chr. 28:19). David also provided materials and money to build the temple to which the leaders and people added their 'freewill offerings'. Exuberant joy filled the givers and the king (1 Chr. 29:1–9). All this took place before David's benediction in 1 Chronicles 29:10–11.

Christians ought to be even more cheerful in their giving because of God's lavish grace (2 Cor. 9:6–9). Cheerful givers give not only their money but also themselves wholeheartedly to God because Christ became poor to make them rich (2 Cor. 8:5, 9).

Why did David want to build a temple? 'The temple would be a place of worship that would bear the name of the Most High; it would be an outward and magnificent sign of Israel's devotion to God.'[4] Today God's temple is not a building but people. We should pray, and work by God's power, for the growth of the spiritual temple (1 Cor.6:19–20; 2 Cor.6:16; Eph.2:19–22; 1 Peter 2:4–10).

David's prayer

We learn from David's prayer (1 Chr. 29:10–19) 'in the presence of all the assembly' (v. 10) about God. He focuses on several of his attributes; it is also a model (especially for those who conduct worship services) of how to pray. David, king of Israel, was subject to a higher King.

David prays to:

THE COVENANT GOD

'David blessed the LORD' (v. 10). This looks back to David's song of praise in chapter 16 (compare 16:36 with 29:10). The name 'LORD' occurs sixteen times in verses 1–22. The Lord is 'the God of Israel' (v. 10); he is 'the God of Abraham, Isaac, and Israel, our fathers' (v. 18). He cared and provided for the patriarchs and for Israel, the nation that grew from their descendants and into which the Messiah, the Saviour of the world, was born. The Lord had put into David's heart this proposal to build a temple and he had moved the people to give generously. Now God would bless this desire and this liberality by giving Solomon wisdom and his helpers the necessary strength and skills to erect 'the house of the LORD' (v. 8).

The Lord, to whom David prayed, saw the afflictions, and heard the groans, of his enslaved people in Egypt. Therefore, he came to rescue them through his servant Moses (Exod. 2:23–25; 3:7–10). We read in Exodus 3 that Moses saw a bush that was 'burning, yet it was not consumed' and that 'God called to him out of the bush' revealing himself as the 'I AM WHO I AM'—the LORD (vv.1–14).

It is usual to pronounce 'LORD' as Jehovah or Yahweh, but in fact we do not know the original enunciation because the Jews concluded from Leviticus 24:16 that it was blasphemous to speak God's name. Therefore, whenever they came across the special covenant name Lord they would use 'Adonai' instead. However, that which is most important to bear in mind about 'the name' is its importance. 'LORD' means that God is eternal and unchanging in his grace and mercy; he is faithful, therefore he never leaves or forsakes believers. He always exists and always cares for them.

Jesus Christ, the Son of the covenant God, sealed the new covenant with his blood when he died on the cross for those given to him by his Father before time (Jer. 31:31–34 with Heb. 8:8–13; 10:15–17; 13:20–21; see also Matt. 26:28; John 17:2, 6, 9 with Rom. 8:28–30; Eph. 1:3–6).

THE ETERNAL GOD

He is 'the God of Israel our father, for ever and ever' (v. 10). In the earlier song David praises God who is 'from everlasting to everlasting' (1 Chr. 16:36). The patriarch, Jacob (deceiver), renamed Israel (struggled with God) after wrestling with God (Gen. 32:22–32), had died many years before David's prayer, but his God lived for ever, and still loved his chosen nation. God delights to call himself 'the God of Jacob' (e.g. Ps. 46:7, 11), because he forgives guilty sinners and he strengthens weak saints.

God is eternal and immutable; by contrast, we are mortal and changing: 'We are strangers before you and sojourners, as all our fathers were. Our days on the earth are like a shadow, and there is no abiding' (1 Chr. 29:15). Life is in a constant state of flux: the innocence of infancy and the energy of youth give way to the responsibilities of adulthood, the pressures of family life and the demands of earning a living. Too often the dreams and ideals of youth evaporate. We discover that nothing on earth provides lasting satisfaction. The years take their toll and the shadow of life is soon gone. Christians are pilgrims who look forward to living for ever with the eternal God in an eternal world of perfect joy.

THE MIGHTY GOD

'Yours, O LORD, is the greatness and the power and the glory and the victory and the majesty, for all that is in the heavens and in the earth is yours. Yours is the kingdom, O LORD, and you are exalted as head above all' (v. 11). Human pride is humbled as the glorious God is adored (v. 13). David's prayer finds an echo in the song of the redeemed in heaven (Rev. 5:11–13).

- Greatness and power. Both words emphasise the supremacy of God the Creator who is the sovereign ruler of the entire universe. He 'rules over all' (v. 12)—nothing happens apart from what he has decreed. 'Both riches and honour' come from him. It is from his hand that the weak receive 'power and might'. He makes some 'great' and 'gives strength to all' (v. 12). Isaiah the prophet spoke of both the gentleness and the greatness of God. The almighty God who created the world carries his people as a tender shepherd carries the young sheep; he graciously gives might and strength to the weak (Isa. 40:11–31).
- Glory. This is the radiance or splendour of God, as seen by Moses (Exod. 33:12–23), Isaiah (Isa. 6:1–13) and three of Jesus' disciples (Peter, James and John) at the Transfiguration (Matt. 17:1–12). We see God's glory in Christ (2 Cor. 4:6). We reveal God's glory by our good deeds (Matt. 5:16). We will reflect God's glory in heaven (Rom. 8:18).
- Victory and majesty. Ungodly rulers and their citizens laugh at God and fight against him and his people. But, 'He who sits in the heavens laughs; the LORD holds them in derision ... He will speak to them in his wrath and terrify them in his fury' (Ps. 2:4–5). It is

better to turn now in genuine repentance to his Son, the King (Ps. 2:6). This is the meaning of Psalm 2:12: 'Kiss the Son, lest he be angry, and you perish in the way.' God's Son, who died to bear his Father's wrath as he bore the sins of those who seek his mercy, is now in heaven: 'he sat down at the right hand of God, waiting from that time until his enemies should be made a footstool for his feet' (Heb. 10:12–13). Every knee will one day bow to Christ, 'every tongue will confess that Jesus Christ is Lord, to the glory of God the Father' (Phil. 2:9–11)—that will be a joyful time for believers but a day of terror for those have rejected God and his beloved Son.

Furthermore, David prays to:

THE GOOD GOD

King David gives all credit to God for the people's remarkable generosity; without him we are nothing and can do nothing: 'Both riches and honour come from you, and you rule over all … For all things come from you, and of your own have we given you … O Lord our God, all this abundance … comes from your hand' (vv. 12, 14, 16; compare James 1:17). This good God who gave his Son, the greatest gift he could give, to save us, will supply all that we really need, spiritually and materially, on our journey to heaven (Rom. 8:32).

THE HOLY GOD

'Your holy name' (v. 16). The holy God tests the heart: 'I know, my God, that you test the heart and have pleasure in uprightness. In the uprightness of my heart I have freely offered all these things, and now I have seen your people, who are present here, offering freely and joyously to you' (v. 17; 1 Chr. 28:9). John MacArthur comments: 'Opportunities for giving to God are tests of the character of a believer's devotion to the Lord. The king acknowledges that the attitude of one's heart is significantly more important than the amount of offering in one's hand.'[5] The Lord looks for uprightness of heart; the upright are those who are sincere, though not yet sinless. Jesus calls the upright 'the pure in heart', who 'hunger and thirst for righteousness' (Matt. 5:6, 8). David was upright; he was a man after God's own heart (1 Sam. 13:14).

When David prayed about God testing the heart, did he recall the Lord's words to Samuel the prophet? 'The Lord sees not as a man sees: man looks on the outward appearance, but the Lord looks on the heart' (1 Sam. 16:7). God rejected disobedient Saul, Israel's first king (1 Sam. 15), and sent Samuel to the family of Jesse, David's father, to anoint a new king. The prophet saw David's seven brothers: each one seemed suitable, but God had not chosen any of them; his choice was the youngest, David the shepherd-boy: 'The Lord said, "Arise, anoint him for this is he"' (1 Sam. 16:12).

The Lord asserted his sovereignty in the choice of Judah rather than one of the other eleven tribes, in picking Jesse's family from all the families of Israel, and selecting David, the youngest son of Jesse, and then in choosing Solomon, instead of David, to build the temple (1 Chr. 28:4–5). Solomon, knowing that God had chosen him, could rest on the promise of his presence: 'Be strong and courageous and do it. Do not be afraid and do not be dismayed, for the Lord God, even my God, is with you. He will not leave you or forsake you, until all the work for the service of the house of the Lord is finished' (1 Chr. 28:20).

Apart from God's grace we would soon wander from the path of holiness. Therefore, David prays, 'O Lord ... keep for ever such purposes and thoughts in the hearts of your people, and direct their hearts towards you' (v.18). In the presence of the holy God we ought, like David, to feel our unworthiness. 'Who am I, and what is my people, that we should be able thus to offer willingly?' (v. 14; 1 Chr. 17:16).

Chapter 8

'Bless the Lord'

The whole assembly joined David in praising God as they humbly 'bowed their heads and paid homage to the Lord and to the king' (v. 20). They worshipped God and honoured the king whom he had given to them. Realising their sinfulness, they offered sacrifices (v. 21): the animals died instead of the people because sin deserves death. These sacrifices which could not remove sin (Heb. 10:4) pointed forward to Christ, God's own Son, the Lamb of God who died to take away sin (John 1:29).

The generosity of the givers (see vv. 6–9) is highlighted again in verse 21, where we read of 'sacrifices in abundance for all Israel.' Every person from every tribe gave willingly and liberally to the Lord. The covenant God of grace is worthy of such praise and such giving. New covenant worshippers devote their lives to the Lord as an expression of their worship. 'By the mercies of God ... present your bodies as a living sacrifice, holy and acceptable to God, which is your spiritual worship' (Rom. 12:1).

The words of verse 22: 'And they ate and drank before the Lord on that day with great gladness' indicate their fellowship with, and confidence before, him. We have even greater access to God through Christ's blood (Eph. 2:18; Heb. 4:14–16; 10:19–22). Jesus Christ, the bread of life, promises the penitent, 'I will come ... and eat with him, and he with me' (Rev. 3:20). Heaven is like an everlasting banquet with Christ the divine bridegroom (Rev. 19:6–9). Will you be among the guests? Will you 'bless the Lord your God' for ever?

NOTES

1 David Brown, *Jamieson-Fausset-Brown Commentary on the Whole Bible* (electronic version, QuickVerse, a division of Findex.inc, Omaha, Nebraska, USA), comments on Matthew 6:13.

2 See Exodus 25:10–22; 37:1–9. I have explained the spiritual significance of the Ark of the Covenant, placed in The Holy of Holies, in my book, *Christ in Exodus* (London: Grace Publications Trust, 2010), pp.112–114.

3 According to Andrew Thomson, Saul became king in 1052 BC, David in 1012 and Solomon in 972. See *Opening up 1 Chronicles* (Leominster: Day One, 2011), p.8. 1 Chronicles was addressed to God's people who had just returned from a seventy-year exile in Babylon. The author of 1 and 2 Chronicles was probably Ezra (compare 2 Chronicles 36:22–23 with Ezra 1:1–4). It was written about 450 BC and was placed at the end of the Hebrew Scriptures.

4 Andrew Stewart, *A Family Tree* (Welwyn Commentary; Darlington: Evangelical Press, 1997), p.17.

5 Stewart, *A Family Tree*, p.203.

A bereaved father's doxology

Job ... fell on the ground and worshipped. And he said, 'Naked I came from my mother's womb, and naked shall I return. The Lord gave, and the Lord has taken away; blessed be the name of the Lord.' (Job 1:21)

'What have I done to deserve this?' Perhaps you've asked that question. Heart-broken Job asked that question too: 'If I sin, what do I do to you, you watcher of mankind? Why have you made me your mark? Why have I become a burden to you? Why do you not pardon my transgression and take away my iniquity? For now I shall lie in the earth; you will seek me, but I shall not be' (Job 7:20–21). Though he was bewildered, angry, and even sometimes sunk into profound depression, nevertheless, he never lost his faith in God. His magnificent doxology at the end of the worst day of his life expressed his faith in God.

Job suffers

Job lived in the land of Uz, a large territory east of the Jordan (Job 1:1). He probably lived some 2,000 years before Christ, about the time of the patriarch Abraham. The author's estimation of Job agrees with God's assessment of his servant (Job 1:, 8; 2:3). Job was 'blameless', which means that he was sincere, even though he was not yet perfect. When God finally speaks from heaven, Job confesses, 'I despise myself, and repent in dust and ashes' (Job 42:6; see also 6:24; 7:21). His friends affirm, 'You are suffering because you are a great sinner.' God says, 'Job's suffering is not because of his sin.' A term closely linked to 'blameless' is 'upright', a word used to describe a road that was straight or level. Job kept on the road of obedience to God. Furthermore, he 'fears God and turns away from evil' (Job 1:8). Fearing God is the hallmark of biblical wisdom: 'The fear of the Lord is the beginning of wisdom, and the knowledge of the Holy One is insight' (Prov. 9:10). This godly man was constantly aware that the holy God knew his thoughts and saw his behaviour. The writer describes Job as 'the greatest of all the people of the east' (Job 1:3); he was a highly respected and influential person. God says: 'There is none like him on the earth' (v. 8). Clearly, he was not suffering because of his personal sin.

Job was evidently a wealthy man, but he did not make a god of his prosperity; rather he used his wealth to provide for his family and to care for the needy. We, like Job, are not 'to set [our] hopes on the uncertainty of riches, but on God, who richly provides us with everything to enjoy'. We are 'to be rich in good works, to be generous and ready to share'; this is to store up heavenly treasure (1 Tim. 6:17–19; Matt. 6:19–21). Rich Job possessed treasure in heaven.

How many people were in Job's family? He was married with ten adult children: seven sons and three daughters (Job 1:2). He prayed for them regularly, but especially after birthday parties, when he accompanied his prayers with 'burnt offerings', one for each of them to atone for any sins they may have inadvertently committed (vv. 4–5). Animals died instead of the children. Job lost his wealth and all his children in one day, but he still praised God: 'The Lord gave, and the Lord has taken away; blessed be the name of the Lord.'

Satan accuses

The scene changes from Job's idyllic home to a heavenly council which results in his life being turned upside down. The writer of Job invites us to attend an unusual council meeting in heaven (Job 1:6–12). 'The sons of God', the angels who sang when God created the world (Job 38:7), attend along with Satan (Job 1:6). He is the leader of the angels who rebelled against God (2 Peter 2:4; Jude 6; Eph. 6:12). The angels, including Satan, 'present themselves before the Lord' to report on their activities and to wait for commissions. The devil is also accountable to God (Job 1:6). In the courtroom of heaven Satan (his name means 'accuser') is the counsel for the prosecution who argues that Job only serves God expecting some reward (vv. 9–11). Despite God's own testimony to Job's character the accuser sneers, 'Does Job fear God for no reason?' (v. 9). Satan suggests that Job's godliness is superficial: 'Stop being good to Job! Send him calamity and he will soon cave in.'

Just as Satan accused Job, so he accuses believers 'day and night' (Rev. 12:10). Nevertheless, God does not listen to these accusations because Christ died to bear our sin and to take on himself God's wrath. Nothing, and nobody, can separate us from God (Rom. 8:33–39). Satan will have no just reason to accuse if we, like Job, are 'blameless and innocent, children of God without blemish'; shining as lights in a depraved world (Phil. 2:15; Matt. 5:14–16). Besides being the accuser, the devil is also the wanderer (Job 1:7; 2:2). It is the picture of a lion preying on unsuspecting victims. He is 'a great red dragon' (Rev. 12:3), and 'a roaring lion', so be on your guard! (1 Peter 5:8–9). He fires 'flaming darts' at the soldiers of Christ (Eph. 6:16).

- Another facet of Satan's personality is that he is the tormentor. In one day ...
- He sent Sabeans to steal the donkeys and oxen and to kill the ploughmen (Job 1:14–15).
- He sent lightning to destroy Job's flock and the shepherds (v. 16).
- He sent Chaldeans to steal the camels and to slaughter the servants (v. 17).
- Worst of all, he sends a howling gale to kill Job's ten children (vv. 18–19).
- Later he afflicts Job with 'loathsome sores from the sole of his foot to the crown of his head' (Job 2:7).

• Then he prompts Job's wife to speak angry words: 'curse God and
die' (Job 2:9).

Worshipping Job triumphs over his tormentor in his doxology, 'The
Lord gave, and the Lord has taken away; blessed be the name of the
Lord', so that 'in all this Job did not sin or charge God with wrong' (Job
1:21–22).

God reigns

Satan is powerful, but God is almighty. 'The Almighty' is one of God's
names used several times in the book of Job (5:17; 6:4, 14; 8:3, 5). It is God
who tells Satan to think about Job (Job 1:8; 2:3). None of Job's suffering
took God by surprise, because he planned it. Nothing happens which he
has not decreed. He is the wise and loving Father who plans everything
for our good (Rom. 8:28). He gives strength to bear what he has planned
because he is 'the Father of mercies and God of all comfort' (1 Cor. 10:13;
2 Cor. 1:3).

God gives Satan permission to afflict Job, though he sets the
boundaries. The sovereign Lord allows the devil to take all that Job has
but not to harm him physically. Shortly afterwards, the devil receives
permission to make Job extremely ill but not to kill him (Job 1:12; 2:6).
God keeps Satan, the ferocious lion, on a chain. God sets the limits for
Satan when he tries and tests us. Death cannot come until God's
appointed time. The devil is not able to do all that he maliciously desires.
Finally, God will throw Satan into the eternal fire of hell (Rev. 20:10).
Meanwhile, he gives us strength to 'resist the devil', so that he flees from
us (James 4:7). At Christ's coming, 'the God of peace' will 'crush Satan
under [our] feet' (Rom. 16:20).

Job praises

Look! What is Job doing? After a horrendous day, 'Job arose and tore his
robe and shaved his head and fell on the ground and worshipped' (Job

1:20). Tearing his robe and falling to the ground expressed his intense grief, something not unusual for the times and the culture of the Middle East. What is extraordinary is that he worships the God who allowed his pain. He does not blame God but adores him. 'Here is a man who is coping with a multiple bereavement. He has been afflicted with loss after loss. His sorrow is real and very great. How difficult it is to worship at such a time! Yet worship is Job's reaction. He is so absorbed by the sovereign action of God in giving and in taking away that there is a humble acceptance in blessing even the hand that has struck him. Would that we could learn to make that our first reaction to crisis—to pray.'[1]

Listen! What is Job saying? 'Naked I came from my mother's womb, and naked shall I return. The Lord gave, and the Lord has taken away; blessed be the name of the Lord' (v.21). Job declares that God has the authority to do whatever he pleases. The gracious provider is sovereign. He has every right to remove the things that he has previously given. Job praises God that he had things to lose in the first place. He goes beyond submission to God's sovereignty and praises him for his goodness. Do you thank God for the material blessings he gives you? Are you grateful to him for all his good gifts? Do you value your family and friends? How easily we take these things, and those we love the most, for granted! Job's attitude annoys Satan, who wants to prove that this righteous man was selfish, serving God only for gain. The opposite was true: Job was God-centred rather than self-centred.

Job asserts that suffering comes from God's hand. Grief-stricken Job knew that God controls all events. To grasp this is like an anchor when the storms of life beat against you. Remember that Job did not know about God challenging the devil and then allowing him to bring severe affliction into his life (Job 1:8; 2:3).

Job's disease

What happened after Job's doxology of praise? More trouble! Imagine you are a doctor and Job is in your surgery. What are his symptoms? Severe itching (Job 2:8), wart-like eruptions (2:7; 7:5), depression (3:1–26; 7:16; 30:15), sleeplessness and nightmares (7:14), crying (16:16), failing vision (16:16), bad breath and rotting teeth (19:17), weight loss (19:20), aching, rotting bones (30:17), peeling skin (30:28, 30) and fever (30:30). He looked so awful that he was repulsive to his wife and his close friends scarcely recognised him (2:12).

To make matters worse his three friends turn up! Their silent presence comforted Job. 'They sat with him on the ground seven days and seven nights, and no one spoke a word to him, for they saw that his suffering was very great.' (2:11–13). But then they began their long-winded speeches and added to Job's distress. David Atkinson sums up the reaction to their friend's suffering: 'They could not live with the human suffering which Job embodied. They had to look for causes. They wanted solutions. They had to search for answers. They were uncomfortable when face to face with that which defied the logic of their own theological position. They had to proclaim the truth. They insisted on treating suffering only as a problem to be solved, rather than being willing to cope with the uncertainty of facing its mystery. And they received a pretty sharp word from the Lord at the end of the day for doing so (see 42:7). This book asks us to walk *with* Job right through the depths of his struggle, open to wherever he takes us, for only so will we catch the significance of the Lord's gracious voice at the story's end.'[2]

To sit silently is often the best comfort to offer those in deep distress. A West Indian woman living in a flat in London received news of her husband's death in a street accident. The shock of the grief stunned her so that she sank into a corner of the sofa and sat there rigid and unhearing. Then the school teacher of one of her children, an English woman, came and sat beside her. Without a word she threw an arm around the tight shoulders, clasping them with her full strength. Tears flowed from the teacher's eyes. And then at last the West Indian woman started to sob. Still not a word was spoken and after a while the visitor got up and left.[3]

Job, aching with agonizing pain, looks forward to living in a perfect body: 'For I know that my Redeemer lives, and at the last he will stand upon the earth. And after my skin has been thus destroyed, yet in my flesh I shall see God, whom I shall see for myself, and my eyes shall behold, and not another' (19:25–27). These are the words of a man who was without the Scriptures to read and without prophets to teach him. They anticipate Paul's teaching in 1 Corinthians 15—Christ's resurrection guarantees our resurrection. The apostle, writing to discouraged believers, says, 'This light momentary affliction is preparing for us an eternal weight of glory beyond all comparison, as we look not to the things that are seen but to the things that are unseen. For the things that are seen are transient, but the things that are unseen are eternal' (2 Cor. 4:17–18). Afflictions are 'light' and 'momentary' compared to the 'eternal weight of glory'; what we see is 'transient' compared to the eternal things which we do not see. The apostle goes on in the next chapter to write about what we do not yet see: the replacing of the temporary tent of this body with the permanent house of the resurrection body, which he describes as 'a building from God, a house not made with hands, eternal in the heavens' (2 Cor. 5:1).

Job's wife's distress

After Job's health broke down his wife said to him, 'Do you still hold fast your integrity? Curse God and die.' (Job 2:9). Don't be too harsh! She was a good wife to Job and their children. She had lost her ten children in one day. That would be enough to devastate any mother. As a mother she may have felt this loss more deeply than Job. The family wealth was gone. She sees her husband screaming with pain on the rubbish tip outside the town where the lepers would go. Furthermore, she feels ill whenever she looks at him and smells his bad breath. She sees her husband sinking into depression. He is dying and she is helpless to relieve his discomfort.

Chapter 9

Her anguish, frustration and anger are hardly surprising in such circumstances. She at least sees things in terms of what God was doing, which is more than can be said of his so-called friends.

What does she mean when she says 'Curse God and die'? Rather than seeing her husband suffering such excruciating pain, she would prefer God to strike him dead and get it over with immediately. Perhaps cursing God would provoke him to kill Job.

Job answers her wisely. 'You speak as one of the foolish women would speak. Shall we receive good from God, and shall we not receive evil?' The author concludes, 'In all this Job did not sin with his lips' (2:10). Though he could not understand God's strange ways he did not think that God acted foolishly. He trusted the all-knowing, all-wise and all-loving God.

Job's joy

At last God speaks to Job. He is angry with Job's friends because 'you have not spoken of me what is right, as my servant Job has'. God instructs Job to offer sacrifices and to pray for them, so that he will not deal with them according to their folly. We read that 'the Lord accepted Job's prayer' (Job 42:7–9)—an anticipation of God forgiving sinners because of Christ who 'always lives to make intercession' for us (Heb.7:25). Job is 'my servant' (42:7–8); he has a special relationship with God.

The book of Job has a happy ending. We read that 'the Lord gave Job twice as much as he had before ... the Lord blessed the latter days of Job more than his beginning' (Job 42:10, 12). God, who took away his ten children, graciously gave him 'seven sons and three daughters', Jemimah, Keziah and Keren-happuch, 'and in all the land there were no women so beautiful as Job's daughters' (vv. 14–15). Job lived to see his great-grandchildren before he died at a ripe old age (v. 16). In this life God does not always give us back what he takes away. Nevertheless, we have God's promise that he will finally amply compensate us for our sufferings: 'For

I consider that the sufferings of this present time are not worth comparing with the glory that is to be revealed to us' (Rom. 8:18).

Praise in pain

Is it possible for modern Christians to praise God in pain? Yes! Jennifer, age 9, went out one day on her bicycle, and never returned. The police found her body a week later in a dam. Her father, a Christian, wrote: 'I was comforted to know that even at that age she was saved, that she was with the Lord.'[4] Here is a bereaved father, like Job, adoring God in his grief.[5] Joni Eareckson Tada, a quadriplegic through a diving accident, speaks of suffering as the intruder who comes knocking at her door. 'He has come for my good, for the good of my character ... real character is more important than temporary comfort.'[6]

Chapter 9

NOTES

1 David Atkinson, *The Message of Job* (Bible Speaks Today; Leicester: Inter-Varsity Press, 1991), pp.23–24.

2 Atkinson, *Job*, pp.15–16.

3 Atkinson, *Job*, p.31.

4 Derek Thomas, *The Storm Breaks* (Welwyn Commentary; Darlington: Evangelical Press, 1995), pp.55–56.

5 Why does God allow children, such as Jennifer, to suffer? There are no easy answers! I would recommend a book that deals frankly and honestly with the problem of suffering: Paul Mallard, *Invest your suffering—unexpected intimacy with a loving God* (Nottingham: Inter-Varsity Press, 2013).

6 Joni Eareckson Tada, quoted by Thomas, *The Storm Breaks*, p.56.

Praise in the book of Psalms

T he book of Psalms is full of benedictions and doxologies. The Jews referred to this part of the Scriptures as 'The Book of Praises', while the Septuagint (the Greek translation of the Old Testament) gave it the title 'The Book of Psalms' from a Greek word indicating songs sung to a musical instrument. The psalter was the hymnal of Jewish worshippers.

The human authors

Who composed these psalms? The main author is David, who wrote at least seventy-five of them; other authors included his son, Solomon (72, 127[1]), Moses (90) and Ethan (89). Psalm 88 is both a psalm of the sons of Korah and a maskil of Herman the Ezrahite. Ten psalms are attributed to the sons of Korah, the temple musicians (42, 44–49, 84–85, 87), and Asaph contributed twelve (50, 73–83). The remaining forty-eight psalms remain anonymous. The Psalms extend from Moses (1410 BC) to the late sixth or early fifth century BC, spanning at least 900 years.

Several of the psalms, such as Psalm 119, the longest of the psalms, employ an alphabetic arrangement to aid memorization. Hywel Jones explains: 'It is a well-known fact that the psalmist used the letters of the Hebrew alphabet as a skeleton for this poem. He assigned one consonant to each section of it in turn, and then opened each line of that section with a word beginning with that consonant. This feature is shown in some English translations by the shape of that consonant being printed above the relevant section as well as its name.'[2] The other acrostic psalms are 9, 10, 25, 34, 37, 111, 112 and 145.

The book of Psalms covers a wide range of human experience, such as sorrow (e.g. 13), depression (e.g. 42), penitence (e.g. 51), thanksgiving (e.g. 103–106), confidence (e.g. 23, 27), wisdom (e.g. 1, 119) and imprecation (the believer praying for God to punish the wicked, e.g. 109). Whatever our circumstances or spiritual condition there is an appropriate psalm to encourage us; they are therefore well loved by believers and have even given comfort to unbelievers. According to Warren Wiersbe, 'There are some four hundred quotations or allusions to the Psalms in the New Testament.'[3]

Historical background

It is useful and interesting to read the psalms within their historical setting, often indicated by the heading, regarded in the Hebrew Scriptures as the first verse. 'What the Hebrew text indicates is that the headings are to be treated as part of God's Word and not ignored or dismissed out of hand. These headings must be clearly distinguished from the attempts in some Bible versions to provide titles to indicate a psalm's content.'[4]

As a case in point, the heading of Psalm 51 links David's prayer of penitence to the visit of Nathan, the prophet, after the king's adultery with Bathsheba. Commentators suggest that Psalm 32 also relates to this event. A good study book will slot the psalms into their probable historical contexts: for example, *Opening up Psalms*, written by Roger Ellsworth and published by Day One.

We ought to read and sing psalms alongside hymns and songs (Eph. 5:19), because they point forward to the coming of the Messiah, the Lord Jesus Christ. Several of the psalms are Messianic, including 2, 8, 16, 20, 21, 22, 23, 24, 31, 35, 40, 41, 45, 50, 55, 61, 68, 69, 72, 89, 97, 102, 109, 110, 118 and 132. We are to shine the light of the New Testament on the pages of the psalms.

Should we sing only psalms?

Those who argue for exclusive psalmody affirm that 'psalms and hymns and spiritual songs' (Eph. 5:19) refer to different types of psalms.

Alternatively, Kenneth Dix, Hebrew scholar and gifted musician, argued, 'From the sacred page of inspired Scripture it *cannot* [his italics] be shown that the expression "psalms, hymns and spiritual songs" is a composite term for the Psalter.' He maintains that the words 'hymns and spiritual songs' are not used in the New Testament to describe 'either a part or the whole of the Book of Psalms'.[5] Each term is a different kind of sacred poetry. Furthermore, we ought to remember that Hebrew poetry does not use the kind of metrical forms we have traditionally in English poetry.

Believers in both Old and New Testaments sang songs other than psalms. Take as examples the songs of Moses and Miriam in Exodus 15, and the songs of Mary and Zachariah in the New Testament (Luke 1:46–55; 67–79). The angels and the redeemed in heaven sing a non-psalm described as 'a new song' (Rev. 5:8–14). The debate will continue! Whether we sing psalms only or also sing other forms of poetry, we should make 'melody to the Lord' from the heart (Eph. 5:19). Sincere praise on the lips flows from redeemed hearts.

Selah

The first occurrence of 'Selah' comes in Psalm 3:2. What does it mean? Hebrew scholar Philip Eveson comments: 'The "Selah" might be a musical direction, indicating an instrumental interlude or pause. In many cases there seems no logical reason for its presence. As with some of the notices in the headings we are at a loss to know precisely what its significance is and why it appears where it does.'[6] This word 'Selah' may indicate a pause for reflection, as suggested by the Amplified Bible: 'Selah [pause, and calmly think of that]!'

Five books

The book of Psalms contains 150 psalms—how then do we select which of them to include in a book on benedictions and doxologies? The choice becomes easier when we realise that Jewish scholars divided the book of

Psalms into five books, each ending with a doxology. We shall focus on each of these doxology psalms. Considering these psalms will present us with a variety of authors and topics.

The five books within the book of Psalms are as follows:

- Book 1: 1–41. The theme of Psalm 41, a psalm of David, is 'Praise the everlasting God.'
- Book 2: 42–72. The theme of Psalm 72, a psalm of Solomon which is Messianic, is 'Praise the glorious King.'
- Book 3: 73–89. The theme of Psalm 89, attributed to Ethan the Ezrahite and the longest of the doxology Psalms, is 'Praise the loving God.'
- Book 4: 90–106. The theme of Psalm 106, the author of which is unnamed, is 'Praise the faithful God.'
- Book 5: 107–150. The theme of the jubilant Psalm 150 (author unknown) is 'Let everything praise God!'

Some biblical scholars think that the five sections of the psalms mirror the five books of the Pentateuch, but I am not convinced that this idea is correct.[7]

Beatitudes

Beatitudes—'blessed are …'—occur in all five books of the Psalms. The Amplified Bible reads: 'Blessed [happy, fortunate, prosperous, and enviable] is the man …' It is clear from Psalm 1 that true blessedness or happiness comes through obeying God's Word. There are twenty-five of these beatitudes altogether:

- Book 1 contains eight: Psalms 1:1; 2:12; 32:1–2; 33:12; 34:8; 40:4; 41:1.
- Book 2 has only one in Psalm 65:4.
- Book 3 has four: Psalm 84:4–5, 12; 89:15.
- Book 4 has two: 94:12; 106:3.

• Book 5 has ten: 112:1; 119:1–2; 127:5; 128:1; 137:8–9; 144:15; 146:5.

Why should we read the psalms?

'The psalms teach us to be much occupied with God. This means we are to treasure his Word, to delight in his worship, to reflect on his glorious attributes, to rehearse his great acts in history, to trust in his care, to glory in his gospel and to anticipate his final victory. The more occupied with God we are, the more strength we find for living.'[8] We delight in worship and occupy ourselves with God as we reflect on the benedictions and doxologies in the psalms.

Comfort for the dying

Dying on the cross, our Lord Jesus Christ drew comfort from, and saw his atoning death as a fulfilment of, the psalms. His cry of dereliction came from Psalm 22:1: 'My God, my God, why have you forsaken me?' (Matt. 27:46). His final words are quoted from Psalm 31:5: 'Father, into your hands I commit my spirit!' (Luke 23:46). The martyr Stephen recalled this same psalm: 'And as they were stoning Stephen, he called out, "Lord Jesus, receive my spirit"' (Acts 7:59). The psalms provide strength for living and comfort for dying.

Chapter 10

NOTES

1 Scholars debate whether these two psalms are about Solomon or written by Solomon. Calvin comments, 'From the inscription of this psalm we cannot determine who was its author. As it is said at the close to be the last words of David's prayer it is more probable that it was composed by him than by Solomon.' *Commentary on the Book of Psalms* (Calvin Translation Society, 1845; repr. Grand Rapids: Baker Book House, 1993), vol. 2.

2 Hywel Jones, *Psalm 119 for life* (Darlington: Evangelical Press, 2009), p.12.

3 Warren Wiersbe, *Be Worshipful—Glorifying God For Who He Is, Psalms 1–89* (ebook; Eastbourne: David C Cook UK; first published Wheaton, Illinois: Victor Books, 2004).

4 Philip Eveson, *Psalms*, vol. 1 (Welwyn Commentary; Darlington: Evangelical Press 2014), p.15.

5 Kenneth Dix, *The Praises of God in Psalms, Hymns and Spiritual Songs* (Burlington, Ontario: Joshua Press, available in the UK from Mayflower Christian Bookshop, Southampton), p.9. Malcolm Watts argues for exclusive psalmody at www.salisburyemmanuel,org,uk. Eveson discusses this issue in *Psalms*, vol. 2 (Welwyn Commentary, Welwyn Garden City, 2015), p.510.

6 Eveson, *Psalms*, vol. 2, p.44.

7 See Hugh Hill, *The Heart of the Bible—what it meant then and what it means now* (Oxford: Monarch Books, an imprint of Lion Hudson, 2013), pp.167–170. Hill deals helpfully with the psalms of imprecation (pp.172–174).

8 Roger Ellsworth, *The Guide—the Bible Book by Book* (Darlington: Evangelical Press, 2002), p.148.

Praise the everlasting God

Blessed be the Lord, the God of Israel, from everlasting to everlasting! Amen and Amen. (Ps. 41:13)

Psalm 41 is the third psalm that begins with 'blessed' (v. 1; see Ps. 1 and Ps. 32). This one also ends with 'blessed' (v. 13). God blesses the believer (v. 1) and the believer responds by blessing God (v. 13). We cannot add to God's glory, but we can express our thankfulness to him in our praise and our godly lives.

'Blessed' comes from a word that means 'to kneel; by implication to bless God (as an act of adoration).' 'Blessed' also signifies 'to be happy' and 'to be pronounced happy'.[1] The Amplified Bible translates, 'Blessed (happy, fortunate, to be envied)'. Do we envy those who have a God-given desire to worship? John MacArthur defines 'blessed' in this way: 'From the perspective of the individual, this is a deep-seated joy and contentment in God; from the perspective of the believing community, it refers to redemptive favour.'[2] True happiness is to worship and to serve God.

David uses this word 'blessed' three times in this psalm. 'Blessed is the one who considers the poor! In the day of trouble the Lord delivers him' (v. 1); the benefactor makes the poor happy. God shows his kindness to those who are kind by delivering them from trouble. Those who know God's kindness are kind to others. This word occurs again in verse 2: 'He [the generous person] is called blessed in the land.' People respect such a person because of his consistent godliness and his unfailing compassion. The third occurrence of this word is in the doxology (v. 13). The psalmist praises God because he is everlasting. The everlasting God is always with us, unchanging in his love and mercy, even when life is tough.

Chapter 11

God is everlasting

The psalmist praises 'the Lord [who is] ... from everlasting to everlasting.'
When we speak of God as everlasting we mean not only that he has no
beginning and no end, but also that he is unchanging. What is true of God
the Father is true of God the Son. This is why the writer to the Hebrews
picks up words from Psalm 102 that describe the everlasting God and
applies them to Christ: 'You, Lord, laid the foundation of the earth in the
beginning, and the heavens are the work of your hands; they will perish,
but you remain; they will wear out like a garment, like a robe you will roll
them up, like a garment they will be changed. But you are the same, and
your years will have no end' (Heb.1:10–12 quoting Ps.102:25–27). God is
'the same'; he does not change even though we change and our
circumstances change. The unchanging God will never fail us.

Why should David specifically offer praise to God for his everlastingness?
Because 'a close friend' whom he 'trusted ... [had] lifted his heel against
[him]' (v. 9; see also Ps. 55:12–14). His 'friendship' was temporary and
insincere. The term 'lifted his heel' suggests that his enemy behaved as if he
had kicked David with a good swing of the foot. Who was this treacherous
friend? It was Ahithophel, who had supported Absalom in his rebellion
against his father. We read this sad story in 2 Samuel 15–18. The events
related in these chapters cover about four years. Nevertheless, David
blesses the Lord his God, whose friendship remains constant and
unchanging. 'God is everlasting' is a theme running throughout Psalm 41.

God's everlasting care

David praises God for his unchanging care in the opening verses of Psalm
41. The psalmist was an example of the caring person whom God blesses.
The Lord had delivered David and restored him to his throne (v. 1). He
had spared David's life despite the malice of his enemies (v. 2). Apparently,
Absalom had taken advantage of David's lingering illness, but God, the
divine physician, had sustained him during that sickness and then

restored him to full health (v. 3). The mighty God's care for David stands in contrast to Absalom's ill-treatment of his frail father. 'The more Satan endeavours to overthrow their [the believers'] faith, and to distract their thoughts, the more should they fix their minds attentively on God alone', comments John Calvin.[3]

The God of David is our God! We too, like David, can look back and see evidence of God's unchanging love. However, we do not look back to live in the past, but to encourage ourselves to trust him in the present and in the future. God has never failed us in the past; he will never simply leave us to cope in our own strength now, nor in the future. The wise God holds our times in his hand (Ps. 31:15). He plans all things for our ultimate good (Rom. 8:28). Our present sufferings pave the road to eternal glory (Rom. 8:17–18; 2 Cor. 5:16–18).

David's response to God's everlasting care is the doxology of Psalm 41:13.

God's everlasting friendship

David's own son, Absalom, and his close friend, Ahithophel, had become his malicious enemies, spreading gossip and slandering his name (vv. 5–9). On the other hand, God had been his unfailing friend and divine protector. It was because God delighted in David that his enemy did not 'shout in triumph' (v. 11).

God the Son, who lived on earth in a human body with a human nature, understands our distress when friends let us down or turn against us. At the Last Supper Jesus, predicting the treachery of Judas, quoted Psalm 41:9; 'He who ate my bread has lifted his heel against me' (John 13:18; compare John 17:12; Acts 1:16). In the Garden of Gethsemane, his closest friends slept and all his disciples deserted him because of fear (Matt. 26:37–46; 56). In the courtyard, later that same night, Peter denied with swearing that he knew Christ (Matt. 26:69–75). On the cross the Son felt forsaken by his Father, so that he cried, 'My God, my God, why have you forsaken me?' (Matt. 27:46). Family and friends may fail us or misunderstand us, but God remains the sympathetic friend. David's response to God's everlasting friendship is the doxology of Psalm 41:13.

God's everlasting grace

Why should David pray twice, 'O Lord, be gracious to me' (vv. 4, 10)? The reason is that he felt, and therefore confessed, his sin: 'for I have sinned against you!' (v. 4). Was he especially thinking of his failure as a father? He had made a rod for his own back in spoiling Absalom. Joab, David's military commander, rebuked the grieving king that he was lamenting the death of his rebel son instead of encouraging his soldiers who had defeated Israel's enemies (2 Sam. 19:1–8).

Perhaps David was also thinking of his adultery with Bathsheba, wife of the brave soldier Uriah the Hittite (2 Sam. 11). His sins were symptoms of a spiritual malady. David, who had been physically unwell, realised that he had a deeper illness—the disease of sin. Only God could heal him (v. 4). We too have this disease. We are all born as sinners (Ps. 51:5, a penitential psalm written about a year after David's adultery). We too must confess our sins to God (1 John 1:9).

In verse 4 the psalmist confesses his sin, yet in verse 12, he writes, 'You have upheld me because of my integrity'. David was not sinless, but he was sincere. He desired to please God though sometimes, like us, he failed.

Did God forgive David? Will he forgive us? Yes! Look at two phrases in verses 11–12: 'you delight in me' and '[you have] set me in your presence for ever'. The almighty and holy God delights in sinners who turn to him in repentance and faith! He welcomes them into his presence. The unchanging God promises to pardon sinners (Isa. 55:6–7). He always keeps his word.

In Christ, and because of his blood, we come near to God. Paul wrote, 'Now in Christ Jesus you who once were far off have been brought near by the blood of Christ ... Through him we both [Jews and non-Jews] have access in one Spirit [the Holy Spirit] to the Father.' The context of these verses reveals that God himself has broken down the barrier of sin that separates us from him and the barriers that divide us from other people (Eph.2:13–18).

Having received forgiveness, we would expect David to forgive his adversaries. Why then does he write: 'Raise me up, that I may repay them!' (v. 10)? This repayment was not personal revenge but his judicial punishment of those who were guilty of treason against him as the God-appointed king of Israel, the nation chosen by God.

David's response to God's everlasting grace is the doxology of verse 13.

God's everlasting covenant

God's everlasting care, friendship and grace flow from his everlasting covenant. He is 'the God of Israel' (v. 13), his people, those whom he chose from before time (Rom. 8:29–30; Eph. 1:3–6). By using this title—'God of Israel'—the psalmist indicates the Lord's everlasting love for his people, which is the source of his unmerited favour towards us. God spoke about this love through the prophet Jeremiah: 'I have loved you with an everlasting love; therefore I have continued my faithfulness to you' (Jer. 31:3). At Calvary, the Lord Jesus Christ, 'the great shepherd of the sheep' shed 'the blood of the eternal covenant' for his sheep (Heb. 13:20).

David praises God (v. 13). The Hebrew name is Elohim and is used in Genesis 1:1: 'In the beginning, God [Elohim] created the heavens and the earth.' The powerful Creator is able to answer our prayers; he is worthy of our praise. Elohim is also 'the Lord', (Jehovah/Yahweh), a name used six times in Psalm 41 (vv. 1–4, 10, 13). He is the covenant God, the great 'I AM WHO I AM', who spoke to Moses at the burning bush (Exod. 3:14). He heard the groans of his enslaved people (Exod. 2:23–24) and sent Moses to deliver them. He saw us in our sin and sent Jesus Christ, his own Son, to redeem us.

'Amen and Amen'

'Amen' is a prayer ('so be it') and an affirmation ('it will be'), because God's promises are true and reliable. The everlasting God keeps his everlasting Word. Why does David repeat the 'Amen'? Calvin explains: 'The term amen is repeated twice, to express the greater vehemence, and that all the godly might be the more effectually stirred up to praise God.'[4] We ought to praise God daily, especially when life is tough, for his care, friendship, and grace that come to us because of his everlasting covenant. We will live for ever to bless our God!

NOTES

1   James Strong, *Strong's Hebrew and Greek Dictionaries* (electronic edition STEP Files © 2003, QuickVerse, a division of Findex.com, Inc.).

2   John MacArthur, *The MacArthur Study Bible NKJV* (Dallas: Word Publishing, 1997), p.743 (note on Psalm 41:1).

3   John Calvin, *Commentary on the Book of Psalms*, vol. 2 (Edinburgh: Calvin Translation Society, 1846; repr. Grand Rapids: Baker Book House, 1993), p.123.

4   Calvin, *Psalms*, vol. 2, p.127.

Praise the glorious King

Blessed be the Lord, the God of Israel, who alone does wondrous things.
Blessed be his glorious name for ever; may the whole earth be filled with his glory!
Amen and Amen! (Ps. 72:18–19)

Scholars debate the authorship of this psalm that closes the second section of the book of Psalms. Should the heading read, 'Of Solomon' (ESV/NIV), i.e., about Solomon, or 'A Psalm of Solomon' (NKJV)? The final verse would seem to indicate that this was David's prayer for his son Solomon: 'The prayers of David, the son of Jesse, are ended' (v. 20). Calvin expressed the view that Solomon turned his father's prayer into a psalm so that it would be 'kept in everlasting remembrance'.[1]

We read in 1 Kings 2:1–3: 'When David's time to die drew near, he commanded Solomon his son, saying, "I am about to go the way of all the earth. Be strong, and show yourself a man, and keep the charge of the Lord your God, walking in his ways and keeping his statutes, his commandments, his rules, and his testimonies, as it is written in the Law of Moses, that you may prosper in all that you do and wherever you turn.' Obedience was the condition of God's promise, 'You shall not lack a man on the throne of Israel' (1 Kings 2:4). David's prayer in Psalm 72 was for the prosperity of Solomon, his successor, and of God's people during his reign. The wise father not only commands his children but prays for them too.

Psalm 72 depicts Solomon at his best; sadly, the young and wise king became a fool in his old age. His love for 'many foreign woman' was his undoing; they turned his heart 'after other gods' (1 Kings 11:1–8). It is evident from 1 Kings 3, where we read that Solomon prayed for wisdom, that his obedience was even then only partial. He married Pharaoh's daughter and allowed the high places that had been associated with idolatry to remain. His disobedience was the reason for the division of his kingdom after his death.

The benediction-prayer of Psalm 72 celebrates the glorious name of King Solomon and, more importantly, the greater name of Jesus the Messiah-King. We see in this psalm several aspects of the glorious name of Solomon and of the even more glorious name of Christ.

Glorious in his justice

David prays for God to give his son justice in verses 1–4 and in verse 14. A just king is impartial in his judgments. He provides for, and defends, the poor. The blood of the oppressed is precious to a righteous king. We too, like the psalmist, ought to pray that civil and spiritual leaders will be people who are fair, honest and godly. Solomon later wrote: 'Righteousness exalts a nation, but sin is a reproach to any people' (Prov. 14:34).

We ought to pray for leaders so 'that we may lead a peaceful and quiet life, godly and dignified in every way'. Godly leaders encourage godliness. Peace within the nation and in churches makes it easier to spread the message of 'God our Saviour, who desires all people to be saved and to come to the knowledge of the truth.' Christ Jesus is the only Mediator for sinners, whatever their social status or ethnic origin (1 Tim. 2:1–5).

The divine King is always just, kind and caring. Human kings and judges can only assess the behaviour of other people; Christ sees the thoughts, intentions and motives behind their conduct. We read about Christ in Isaiah 11:3–5: 'He shall not judge by what his eyes see, or decide disputes by what his ears hear, but with righteousness he shall judge the poor, and decide with equity for the meek of the earth; and he shall strike the earth with the rod of his mouth, and with the breath of his lips he shall kill the wicked. Righteousness shall be the belt of his waist, and faithfulness the belt of his loins.'

The words of the same prophet, Isaiah, were on the gracious Saviour's lips at the beginning of his public ministry: 'The Spirit of the Lord GOD is upon me, because the Lord has anointed me to bring good news to the poor; he has sent me to bind up the broken-hearted, to proclaim liberty to the captives, and the opening of the prison to those who are bound' (Isa. 61:1–2; Luke 4:16–20). Matthew quotes Isaiah's prediction of the gentle Messiah: 'A bruised reed he will not break, and a faintly burning wick he will not quench; he will faithfully bring forth justice. He will not grow faint or be discouraged till he has established justice in the earth' (Isa. 42:3–4; Matt. 12:15–21). Believers receive these blessings because the wicked treated Christ unfairly, and cruelly nailed him to a cross where 'he was wounded for our transgressions [and] crushed for our iniquities' (Isa. 53:5).

Glorious in his eternity

Verses 5, 7 and 17 can only be true of Christ, who is eternal. Though he died like Solomon, yet, unlike that king, he rose from the dead and is alive for evermore (Rev. 1:18). People feared Solomon in the sense that they respected him because of his wise leadership; we adore Christ the king because he is God who came to earth to redeem us from sin. Solomon was mortal, Christ will live for ever; we will praise his name without ceasing. Sinners from all the nations of the world will adore him.

The mention of 'his name' (v. 17) finds an echo in Philippians 2. Christ's exaltation (Phil. 2:9–11) was the reward—notice the word 'Therefore' in verse 9—of his humiliation (Phil. 2:5–8). He who 'made himself nothing, taking the form of a servant' was 'highly exalted' by God and given 'the name that is above every name, so that at the name of Jesus every knee should bow' and so that 'every tongue [should] confess that Jesus Christ is Lord, to the glory of God the Father'.

What does Paul mean by the phrase, 'the name that is above every name'? Calvin comments: 'The meaning ... is that supreme power was given to Christ, and that he was placed in the highest rank of honour, so that there is no dignity found in heaven or in earth that is equal to his.'[2] David Chapman, an American professor, comments: 'When Jesus receives the "name that is above every name", we again witness His returning to the position of honour and glory He possessed as one who was "equal with God" (2:6), for truly God alone possesses such a "name!"'[3]

Glorious in his compassion

David highlights Solomon's compassion in verses 12–14. He desires that his son will have a long life in which to show kindness to his citizens, that he will receive a grateful reward and that his people will pray continually for him (v. 15). He also prays for abundant harvests and that the fame of Solomon might spread far and wide (vv. 16–17). Civil and spiritual leaders ought to value the prayers of God's people.

The heavenly Monarch excels Solomon in his compassion. Three of the Gospel writers often highlight Jesus' compassion: for example, 'When he saw the crowds, he had compassion for them, because they were harassed and helpless, like sheep without a shepherd'; 'I have compassion on the crowd, because they have been with me now three days and have nothing to eat'; 'And when he Lord saw her [the widow of Nain], he had compassion on her and said to her, "Do not weep"' (Matt. 9:36; Mark 8:2; Luke 7:13). His pity always led to action: dying for the lost sheep, feeding the hungry crowd and giving life to the widow's dead son. John does not focus so much on Jesus' compassion because he majors on his deity. It is true that he tells the story of the miraculous feeding of five thousand people (John 6:1–13), but he does so to prove that Jesus is the bread of life. The 'I am' sayings in John's Gospel recall the 'I AM THAT I AM' who spoke to Moses from the burning bush (Exod. 3:14).

Glorious in his fame

David prays, 'may the whole earth be filled with his glory!' (v. 19). Solomon's kingdom stretched over a vast amount of land. 'The River' referred to in verse 8 is the Euphrates. Kings and queens, including the Queen of Sheba, travelled great distances to see Solomon and to test his wisdom (vv. 8–11, 15; 1 Kings 10). The righteous flourished throughout his long and peaceful reign (v. 7).

The fame of Solomon is nothing compared with the glory of God 'who alone does wondrous things' (v. 18). Some of these 'wondrous things' included creating a world from nothing in six days, by merely speaking; dividing the Red Sea; sustaining his chosen people for forty years in an inhospitable desert; and protecting the Jewish race so that from that people the Messiah-Saviour would be born. The greatest of the Lord's 'wondrous things' was Christ dying on a cross to save a vast multitude of sinners from all the nations of the world (Rev.7:9–10).

Christ's dominion covers the world—not just an area of the Middle East—and his citizens—the redeemed—come from every age of history and from every nation to serve him (Ps. 72:8–11). Solomon died and his kingdom was torn in two: the ten tribes of Israel in the north and the two tribes of Judah in the south. The glory of the eternal King, who created the earth (v. 6), the moon (v. 5) and the sun (v. 17), will last for ever. No one can destroy his kingdom or thwart his sovereign decrees; rather, all will 'bow down before him, and his enemies [will] lick the dust!' (v. 9). Verse 7 will have its complete fulfilment when Christ comes to reign on the new earth, the final home of God's people (2 Peter 3:13). Then, 'the whole earth'—not just the land of Israel—'[will] be filled with his glory' (v. 19; Isa. 11:9; Hab. 2:14).

Present salvation and future blessings flow from God's grace; he is 'the Lord, the God of Israel', who made a covenant to save those whom he gave, in eternity, to his Son, and for whom Christ died at Calvary. Everyone for whom he died will reach heaven by the mighty power of

God (John 6:37–40; 10:16–18, 28–30; 17:2, 6, 9, 11–12, 24; Rom. 8:28–39; 1 Peter 1:5). Meanwhile, we ought, like David, to praise God: 'Blessed be his glorious name for ever ... Amen and Amen!' (v. 19).

NOTES

1 John Calvin, *Commentary on the Book of Psalms*, vol. 2 (Edinburgh: Calvin Translation Society, 1846; repr. Grand Rapids: Baker Book House, 1993), Introduction to Psalm 72.

2 John Calvin, *Commentaries on the Epistles of Paul: Galatians to Philemon* (Edinburgh: Calvin Translation Society; repr. Grand Rapids: Baker Book House, 1993), pp.60–61.

3 See David Chapman's discussion of the 'name' in *Philippians—Rejoicing and Thanksgiving*, (Fearn, Ross-shire: Christian Focus, 2012), pp.136–137.

Praise the loving God

Blessed be the Lord for ever! Amen and Amen. (Ps. 89:52)

A man is in the sea after a strong wave has caused his small, lightweight sailing boat to capsize and break up. He clings desperately to planks of wood from the boat. He needs something to keep him from sinking for ever into the depths of the sea. Sometimes life seems like a capsized boat. We feel overwhelmed by circumstances beyond our control. We need something to cling on to; something to give us stability in the raging sea of life.

Ethan, the author of Psalm 89, and the nation of Israel, the people of God, were in a storm of suffering. To paraphrase the psalmist's lament in verses 38–51: 'God has abandoned us and allowed our enemies to defeat us; they are laughing at us. You, God, have hidden yourself. It seems as if you no longer love your people. It looks as if you have broken your promises. Worse still, our enemies are mocking you, our God.' Despite this situation, the psalmist still praises God in the doxology that ends the third book of the Psalms (v. 52).

Who was this Ethan? Commentators debate his identity. He probably lived at the time of Jehoiachin, who became king of Judah at the age of eighteen. Sadly, he only reigned three months before the armies of Nebuchadnezzar marched into Jerusalem and took the young king captive to Babylon (2 Kings 24:8–17). If Psalm 89:45 is a reference to this event, that would explain the lament of verses 38–51. 'Maybe, like some of the psalms attributed to Asaph, it was composed by a member of Ethan's family who lived after the events of 587 BC'[1] when the nation was taken into exile.

Distressed Ethan reminds himself of God's love, faithfulness and power.

God's love

Two of God's attributes sustained Ethan in life's storms: his steadfast love and his persistent faithfulness. 'I will sing of the steadfast love of the Lord, for ever; with my mouth I will make known your faithfulness to all generations' (v. 1). Like a recurring motif in a piece of music these twin themes are heard several times in Psalm 89—see verses 1–2, 14, 24, 28 and 49.

What is God's steadfast love? We read in verse 1 that his love is 'steadfast', which means that it is unchanging. This 'steadfast love will be built up for ever' (v. 2): God's love for his people is everlasting. His love never changes or ceases, though sometimes circumstances cause us to doubt his love, so that we ask, 'Lord, where is your steadfast love of old?' (v. 49). The God of steadfast love and faithfulness is the 'Lord' (Jehovah/ Yahweh) (v. 1)—this name occurs nine times in the psalm. He is the caring God who saw the suffering of his afflicted people and commissioned Moses, at the burning bush, to rescue them (Exod. 3:7–10; 4). He heard the lament of his exiled people who felt abandoned by their God (Ps. 89:38–51). He knows our sorrows too! He gives comfort and strength to those who seek him at his throne of grace (Heb. 4:14–16).

God's faithfulness

What is God's faithfulness? It means that he never breaks the promises which he has given to us in his Word. His faithfulness is 'in the heavens' (v. 2): it is as fixed and enduring as the sun and moon. Faithfulness is an essential part of God's character: 'Your faithfulness [is] all around you' (v. 8). He is always faithful; constantly reliable and trustworthy.

God revealed his faithfulness in the covenant that he made with David (2 Sam. 7). He made this special agreement when David wanted to build a permanent house for God in which to place the Ark of the Covenant, the symbol of God's presence. Instead of allowing David to erect a temple, God speaks of building for David a permanent 'house', a dynasty (2 Sam. 7:11).

The Lord appointed Solomon, David's son, to build a 'house' for God, the temple in Jerusalem. God kept his promises! (1 Kings 5–9). The Lord appointed Solomon, David's son, to build a 'house' for God, the temple in Jerusalem. God kept his promises (1 Kings 5–9)! We read in verses 19–27 about the promises of God's covenant and in verses 28–37 about the permanence of his covenant.

It was God who chose David and sent Samuel to anoint him as Israel's king (vv. 19–20). God would strengthen him to defeat his enemies (vv. 19–25). David prayed, 'You are my Father, my God, and the Rock of my salvation' (v. 26). Christ also prayed to 'my God' and 'my Father' and committed himself to 'the Rock of my salvation' (who delivered him from the darkness of the tomb) (Matt. 26:39, 42; 27:46; John 20:17; Heb. 5:7; 1 Peter 2:23).

David was God's 'firstborn, the highest of the kings of the earth' (v. 27). The firstborn son enjoyed distinctive privileges and responsibilities in a Jewish family. David is a type of Christ. Paul describes him as 'the firstborn of all creation' and 'the firstborn from the dead'—the pre-eminent Son in whom the fulness of God dwelt when he walked on earth in a human body (Col. 1:15, 18–19; 2:9). He is 'the firstborn from the dead, and the ruler of kings on earth', now enthroned in heaven (Rev. 1:5; Phil. 2:9–11; Eph. 1:15–23). Christians, God's children, belong to 'the assembly of the firstborn' (Heb. 12:23). God will 'transform our lowly body to be like his glorious body' (Phil. 3:20–21; 1 Cor. 15:50–57).

Would God's covenant still stand if David's children sinned against him? God would discipline them—their present suffering was evidence of this fact—but he could never break his covenant (vv. 30–35). God has made a covenant with his people, Christians, to save them completely;

nothing, not even their sins, can thwart his eternal plans (Rom. 8:28–30; Heb. 7:25). He disciplines his children (Heb. 12:3–11), but never abandons them (Heb. 13:5–6; Rom. 8:31–39). God's genuine children repent of their sins and aspire to love and obey him, though painfully aware of the inadequacy of their devotion. God's love is never-ending and unchangeable!

How are we to understand God's pledge, 'I will establish his offspring for ever and his throne as the days of the heavens' (v. 29), and, 'His offspring shall endure for ever, his throne as long as the sun before me. Like the moon it shall be established for ever, a faithful witness in the skies' (vv. 36–37)? David is dead and his dynasty in Israel no longer exists. Has God broken his promises? These promises anticipate the coming of a greater than David, the Lord Jesus Christ.[2]

The prophet Isaiah predicted the birth of a child, a son, whose name would be 'Wonderful Counsellor, Mighty God, Everlasting Father, Prince of Peace.' His 'government of peace' would have no end; he would sit 'on the throne of David ... for evermore' (Isa. 9:6–7). He is Immanuel—God with us—born from the womb of a virgin (Isa. 7:14). 'The angel of the Lord', who appeared to Joseph in a dream, identified Jesus as the Immanuel, son of a virgin, spoken of in Isaiah's prophecy (Matt. 1:20–23). The prophet predicted Jesus' birth and death some 700 years before these events.

Four chapters later Isaiah wrote: 'There shall come forth a shoot from the stump of Jesse [David's father], and a branch from his roots shall bear fruit' (Isa. 11:1). Later he wrote about this same person growing up 'like a young plant, and like a root out of dry ground', an unattractive plant from the decaying tree of the royal family of David (Isa 53:2). This root/branch is the Lord Jesus Christ.

When the angel Gabriel appeared to a frightened virgin named Mary he said, 'Behold, you will conceive in your womb and bear a son, and you shall call his name Jesus. He will be great and will be called the Son of the

Most High. And the Lord God will give to him the throne of his father David, and he will reign over the house of Jacob for ever, and of his kingdom there will be no end' (Luke 1:30–33). Mary's Son, Jesus, would sit on David's throne! God was about to fulfil his promises to David. Christians, whether they are Jewish or non-Jewish, are citizens of God's everlasting kingdom (Gal. 3:26–29). This is something for which we ought to bless the Lord (Ps. 89:52)! We may say then that 'God did not violate his covenant, he fulfilled it more gloriously than in a mere succession of descendants of David, most of whom were unDavidlike anyway!'[3]

God's power

Besides recalling God's love and faithfulness, Ethan also reminds himself that God is the incomparable king of the entire universe who rules with righteousness and justice and is the defender of his people (vv. 5–18). The divine King is awesome (v. 7). Today the word 'awesome' is misused and overused. We ought to consider the might and greatness of God; he really is awesome. We have proof that God is awesome in his subduing of the seas, one of his first acts of creation (v. 9; Gen. 1:2, 6–10).

A further display of God's power was the scattering of the armies of Pharaoh in the Red Sea (vv. 9–10). Rahab (v. 10) was 'the monster of the sea, also called "Leviathan", possibly Sobek, who was the crocodile god. Rahab's subjects, the Egyptians, invaded God's people. But Ethan recalls how God had *crushed* them when he struck the Nile and later overthrew them in the Red Sea.'[4]

Responding to God's love and faithfulness

How should we bless the Lord for his love and faithfulness?

1) PRAISE GOD

'I will sing of the steadfast love of the Lord, for ever' (v. 1). God's steadfast love is 'for ever' (compare v. 28); it began before time, will be unchanging in time and will continue beyond time into eternity. Praise God that there is nothing and no one who can separate us from his love. We ought frequently to reflect on Jeremiah 31:3; Romans 8:28–39; Ephesians 1:3–14 and 3:14–21. God's love is far greater than we will ever understand, even in heaven, when we shall see the God of matchless love face to face (1 John 3:1–3; Rev. 22:4)!

We praise God that he is faithful even when we are unfaithful. It was because of Israel's unfaithfulness that they were suffering. The faithful God forgives his unfaithful people (Micah 7:18–20)

Our praise should be ...

Public

Ethan composed this psalm for believers to sing when they met for worship. Collectively we adore God, whose love, faithfulness and power are eternal and unchanging. As we worship we encourage fellow-believers. 'Let us consider how to stir up one another to love and good works, not neglecting to meet together, as is the habit of some, but encouraging one another, and all the more as you see the Day drawing near' (Heb. 10:24–25). 'The Day' anticipates Christ coming, when we shall praise God with sinless souls in glorified bodies.

Determined

Ethan says, 'I will sing ... I will make known' (v. 1). Though the people have broken hearts and tearful eyes, the psalmist calls on them to sing about God's love. Paul and Silas in the prison at Philippi sang hymns at midnight (Acts 16:25)!

Enthusiastic

Look at verse 15: 'Blessed are the people who know the festal shout ['joyful sound', NKJV], who walk, O Lord in the light of your face.' 'The festal shout' may refer to the shout of a victorious army or to the joy of pilgrims when they celebrated the religious feasts; maybe it alludes to the blowing of the trumpet in the year of jubilee when Hebrew slaves were freed (Lev. 25). We are soldiers and pilgrims because God has set us free by the blood of Christ. He became a servant to deliver us from bondage to Satan and sin (Phil. 2:4–8).

Those who joyfully worship God are 'blessed'; they are truly happy and to be envied. Those who sincerely worship God 'walk ... in the light of [his] face'; they enjoy fellowship with him and experience his favour. The phrase 'in the light of your face' echoes the Aaronic benediction of Numbers 6:24–26.

Constant

We are to praise God constantly: 'the people ... exult in your name all the day and in your righteousness are exalted' (v. 16). We adore him not only in the place of worship but every day by offering to him our lives as 'a living sacrifice' (Rom. 12:1). Albert Barnes comments on the second part of verse 16: 'The effect of that knowledge shall be to exalt or to elevate them in moral character, in happiness, in the esteem of others, and in true prosperity.'[5]

2) TALK ABOUT GOD

'... with my mouth I will make known your faithfulness to all generations' (v. 1). The word 'mouth' brings to mind Romans 10:9–10: 'If you confess with your mouth that Jesus is Lord and believe in your heart that God raised him from the dead, you will be saved. For with the heart one believes and is justified, and with the mouth one confesses and is saved'. May we not say that verbal confession points toward the sincerity and genuineness of an inner faith? Allowing for different temperaments (some are shy and others more outgoing), a reluctance to speak may indicate a lack of real saving faith. An aspect of acknowledging 'Jesus is Lord' is an eagerness to serve him.

3) FEAR GOD

God is 'a God greatly to be feared in the council of the holy ones' (v. 7). These 'holy ones' are 'the heavenly beings' (v. 6), and the 'hosts' (v. 8)—a vast angelic army who swiftly perform his will. We too should willingly obey him (Matt. 6:10). What is this fear of God (v. 7)? It means 'to recognise him for who he truly is. Fearing him is not about being terrified of him. It is about knowing that he is the God who made the world, rules the world and will judge the world, and so giving him the reverential respect and honour that are his due.'[6]

Adoring God

The word 'blessed' means to kneel in adoration before God. The almighty and awesome God of steadfast love and faithfulness is worthy of our praise. No wonder that Ethan repeats his final 'Amen' (v.52)!

NOTES

1 Philip Eveson, *Psalms*, vol. 1 (Welwyn Commentary; Darlington: Evangelical Press 2014), p.121.

2 Malcolm Jones deals with the 'For ever' promises in the Old Testament: *Abraham's People—A biblical introduction to the people of God, their identity and future* (Leominster: Day One Publications, 2015), appendix 2, pp.57–62. I would recommend this simple-to-read book; it packs so much into 62 pages!

3 Lane, *Psalms 1–89: the Lord saves* (Fearn, Ross-shire: Christian Focus, 2006), p.395.

4 Eric Lane, *Psalms 1–89*, p.392 [Lane's italics].

5 Albert Barnes, *Notes on the Old Testament*. I have Barnes' Notes as part of the QuickVerse 8 Bible Software (Parsons Technology Inc., Cedar Rapids, Iowa).

6 Jonathan Griffiths, *Wholeheartedness: the Message of Haggai for Today* (Leominster: Day One, 2014), p.33.

Praise the faithful God

Praise the Lord! Oh give thanks to the Lord, for he is good, for his steadfast love endures for ever! ... Blessed be the Lord, the God of Israel, from everlasting to everlasting! And let all the people say, 'Amen!' Praise the Lord! (Ps. 106:1, 48)

This psalm, whose composer is unknown, runs to forty-eight verses and closes the fourth section of the Psalter. As we have seen, each of the five sections of the book of Psalms ends with a doxology. This psalm begins and concludes with 'Praise the Lord!' (vv. 1, 48).

Psalms 105 and 106 are 'twin psalms', similar but not identical. Both psalms trace Israel's history: the first, to reveal that the faithful God kept his promises to Abraham; the second, to focus on the unfaithfulness of Israel. Parts of Psalm 106 are similar to the song of thanksgiving which was uttered when the ark arrived in Jerusalem (compare verses 1 and 47–48 with 1 Chronicles 16:34–36).

Praise

The psalmist calls upon us to 'Praise the Lord!' We are to praise him because 'he is good' and because 'his steadfast love endures for ever' (v. 1). In contrast to the nation's faithlessness—and ours—God's goodness and love are constant and unchanging. Our praise for God's 'mighty deeds' is inevitably inadequate, but, nevertheless, should always be sincere (v. 2). Those who genuinely praise God are just and righteous; they show God's goodness and love to others (v. 3). Sadly, these qualities were too often lacking throughout Israel's history. Isaiah complained that 'he looked for justice, but behold, bloodshed'; he also looked 'for righteousness, but behold, an outcry!' (Isa. 5:7). God looked at Israel his vineyard and saw

Chapter 14

bad fruit. Does God see in us 'the fruit of the Spirit' (Gal. 5:22–23)? Worship without godliness is hypocrisy.

Prayer

Praise (vv. 1–3) leads to prayer (vv. 4–5). In every situation we ought to pray, 'Remember me, O Lord' (v. 4). This was the prayer of blind Samson when he prayed for strength to defeat the Philistines, the oppressors of God's people (Judg. 16:28). It was also the prayer of barren Hannah when she prayed for a son, whom she promised to give back to God (1 Sam. 1:11). Furthermore, this prayer was on the lips of the penitent thief who asked the dying Saviour for pardon (Luke 23:42).

God's people are 'your chosen ones' who look forward to 'your inheritance' (Ps. 106:5). In Christ, Jews and non-Jews are God's 'chosen race, a royal priesthood, a holy nation, a people for his own possession' (1 Peter 2:9), who look forward to 'an inheritance that is imperishable, undefiled, and unfading' (1 Peter 1:4).

As the psalmist prayed for 'the prosperity' of Israel, so we should entreat him for his blessing on the church in the growth of believers and the conversion of unbelievers. Our prayers should be joyful, 'that I may rejoice in the gladness of your nation' (Ps. 106:5). Praise and prayer belong together!

Confession

When we come to the holy God with praise and in prayer we soon become aware of our sinfulness. The psalmist includes himself as he confesses the present and past sins of the nation. 'Both we and our fathers have sinned; we have committed iniquity; we have done wickedness' (v. 6). This prayer recalls that of Solomon when the ark was brought to Jerusalem (1 Kings 8:47), and is echoed by Daniel when sinful Israel was exiled in Babylon (Dan. 9:5; see also Neh. 9).

It was not long after leaving Egypt that the people forgot God's steadfast love and rebelled at the Red Sea (Ps. 106:7). Nonetheless, God delivered them from their adversaries when he drowned Pharaoh's army (vv. 8–11). God rescued his recalcitrant people 'for his name's sake' to 'make known his mighty power' (v. 8). This was an extraordinary display of the faithful God's goodness, steadfast love and strength. His power was acknowledged by Israel and by the enemy: 'Israel saw the great power that the Lord used against the Egyptians, so the people feared the Lord, and they believed in the Lord and in his servant Moses' (Exod. 14:31, see also verses 14 and 18 in this chapter).

Grumbling

The fear of God (in the verse quoted above), believing his words and the song of praise (Ps. 106:12; Exod. 15:1–21) were quickly replaced by grumbling about the Lord's provision in the wilderness, which led to railing against Moses and Aaron, the God-appointed leaders (Ps. 106:13–15; Exod. 15:22–25; 16:2–3; 17:1–7; Num. 11:1–15, 31–35; 14:1–12). Yet, despite their complaining, God continued to feed them with manna and quails and reveal his glory to them (Exod. 16:9–12). He gave them what they wanted, but it cost their lives (Ps. 106:15).

Another example of their peevishness occurs in Psalm 106:16–18, in which we read about the mutiny led by Dathan (Num. 16). God punished the mutineers by the earth swallowing them and fire burning the wicked. Grumbling is not just a sin of God's people in the Old Testament. The apostle Paul tells the church at Philippi to 'do all things without grumbling' (Phil. 2:14). The antidote to grumbling is to 'rejoice in the Lord always'—a command issued twice in one verse—and to pray. God gives his peace to his praying and praising people (Phil. 4:4, 7).

Idolatry

Soon after God gave Israel the Ten Commandments, forbidding the worshipping of other gods and making images to represent him (Exod.

20:1–21), the people worshipped a golden calf (Ps. 106:19–23; Exod. 32). The heinousness of this transgression is highlighted in verses 20–22: they 'exchanged the glory of God for the image of an ox that eats grass' (compare Rom. 1:23); this was to forget 'God, their Saviour', who displayed his awesome power in the plagues in Egypt and by parting the Red Sea for some two million people. God threatened to destroy Israel, but Moses 'stood in the breach' (Ps. 106:23)—he entreated the faithful God to show mercy to the defiant.

The incident of Moses interceding for the sinful nation is found in Exodus 32. Moses was on Mount Sinai, receiving the Ten Commandments engraved by God's own finger on two tablets of stone. Below the mountain the people danced before a golden calf! God says to Moses, 'Let me alone, that my wrath may burn hot against them and I may consume them, in order that I may make a great nation of you.' Instead of accepting this offer of greatness, Moses implores the Lord to spare his people lest the Egyptians deride God. He also reminds God of his promises to Abraham, Isaac and Jacob to make their descendants more numerous than the stars and the grains of sand (Exod. 32:8–14). The next day, Moses prays again, offering his own life for the sinful nation: '"... forgive their sin—but if not, please blot me out of your book that you have written." But the Lord said to Moses, "Whoever has sinned against me, I will blot out of my book"'. He sends a plague to punish the transgressors (Exod. 32:30–35).

Thankfully, in the person of our Lord Jesus Christ, we have a greater advocate than Moses to intercede on our behalf before the Father's throne of grace. Moreover, though our sins undoubtedly deserve God's wrath, it is because of the irresistible merit of Christ's perfect righteousness and sacrificial death that we are spared (Rom. 8:32). He died to bear our sin and make it possible that sinners like us might have an all-sufficient advocate before the Father (1 John 2:1–2)! Moses' death could not blot out the sin of a guilty nation; but Jesus Christ could not only ensure that verdicts of 'not guilty' and 'perfectly righteous' are imputed to us, but that all that is necessary has been done to guarantee that the name of every true believer is inscribed in God's eternal book of life!

Disobedience

God promised to the Hebrews 'the pleasant land' (Ps. 106:24), Canaan, a land that 'flows with milk and honey' (Num. 13:27). But 'they murmured in their tents, and did not obey the voice of the Lord' (Ps. 106:25). They listened to the discouraging report of the ten spies about giants in the land rather than listening to God's voice (Num. 13:25–33). The outcome of this unbelief was that those who left Egypt perished in the wilderness (Ps. 106:26–27). The raised hand (v. 26) was an ancient gesture for swearing an oath: see, for example, Abram's words to Melchizedek, the king of Sodom (Gen. 14:22). The words 'scattering them among the lands' (Ps. 106:27) look beyond the wilderness wanderings to the seventy-year exile in Babylon. This was a punishment for Israel's disobedience: 'If ... you will not listen to me, but walk contrary to me, then I will walk contrary to you ... and I myself will discipline you sevenfold for your sins ... I will lay your cities waste ... I myself will devastate the land ... I will scatter you among the nations ...' (Lev. 26:27–33). Psalm 106 probably dates from the time of the exile; the deportees knew the painful consequences of violating God's law.

A further illustration of Israel's unfaithfulness comes from near the end of their forty-year stay in the wilderness. On the border of Canaan they joined 'Baal of Peor' (Ps. 106:28–31). Numbers 25 tells the sad story. Peor was a mountain in Moab, east of the Dead Sea, where the people worshipped Baal. This time it was Phinehas, grandson of Aaron, who intervened to prevent God wiping out the whole race with a plague (Ps. 106:30). This appeal was 'counted to him as righteousness', a phrase that recalls Genesis 15:6, and springs us into Paul's letter to the Romans (see especially chapter 4). God acquits those who repent because he declared the sinless Christ guilty in our place.

The never-ending petulance became too much for Moses (known for his meekness, Num. 12:3), who had offered his own life to God for the nation (Ps. 106:23). He spoke rashly when he struck the rock in anger. Moses' rashness deprived him of the privilege of leading the people into Canaan (Ps. 106:32–33; Num. 20:1–13).

Was God being too harsh with Moses, who had faithfully served him despite rejection by those whom he had led for forty years? No, because his conduct was a symptom of his unbelief. 'You did not believe in me' was God's charge against Moses when he struck the rock instead of commanding water to come from it. His anger against God's people reflected badly on God's name; it dishonoured his holy name (Num. 20:12). The gracious God gave the rebels water from the rock. Spiritual leaders should be caring and patient towards God's people (1 Thess. 5:14).

In contrast to Moses, 'when [Jesus] was reviled, he did not revile in return; when he suffered, he did not threaten, but continued entrusting himself to [God] who judges justly'. This attitude paved the way to the cross where he 'bore our sins in his body'. Peter refers to Jesus' non-retaliation as confirmation that he 'committed no sin' and as an example for believers, especially the oppressed, to 'follow in his steps' (1 Peter 2:18–25).

Unfaithfulness

In Psalm 106:34–41 we follow the Israelites into Canaan, where they intermarried into idol-worshipping families and even sacrificed their children to these false gods. God viewed this as spiritual adultery. The divine husband punished his unfaithful wife by allowing enemies to tyrannize his people, such as in the time of the Judges. The faithful God 'many times … delivered them'; he 'looked upon their distress, when he heard their cry' (vv. 42–44). The Lord 'does not deal with us according to our sins, nor repay us according to our iniquities' (Ps. 103:10).

Why was God faithful to such an unfaithful nation? It was because 'he remembered his covenant, and relented according to the abundance of his steadfast love' (v. 45). Israel's disloyalty could not prevent God fulfilling his promises to Abraham that through his descendants blessing would flow beyond the Jewish nation to the world; from that nation came the Messiah, the Saviour of the world. The phrase 'abundance of his steadfast love' (v. 45; see also v. 7) anticipates the aged John's amazement at God's generous love: 'How great is the love the Father has lavished on us, that we should be called children of God' (1 John 3:1, NIV). Does verse 46 recall Cyrus' decree that the exiled Jews should return to their land (Ezra 1)? The following verse is clearly a prayer for the Lord to bring his people back to their land; a prayer that would cause them to 'give thanks to your holy name and glory in your praise' (v. 47).

Amen!

The faithful God who is 'from everlasting to everlasting' is everlasting in his love and compassion towards us. We shall adore him eternally for his undeserved love! 'Amen'—a prayer, 'may it be', and an affirmation, 'it will be'—is an appropriate conclusion to the fourth book of Psalms. It is an apt word for a congregation to use at the end of worship, 'Let all the people say "Amen!" Praise the Lord!' (v. 48).

This long psalm comes full circle and ends as it began with the call to 'Praise the Lord' (vv. 1, 46). It is a psalm that encourages believers to remember God's promises and to rejoice in his unchanging love in all the changing circumstances of their lives. He is the faithful God who never breaks his word.

'Let everything that has breath praise the LORD!'

Praise the Lord! ... Let everything that has breath praise the Lord! Praise the Lord!
(Ps. 150:1, 6)

The book of Psalms ends with an ecstatic song of praise. This word 'praise' occurs thirteen times in six short verses; an appropriate doxology with which to close the psalter. Psalms 146 to 150 begin and end with the words, 'Praise the Lord!' The Hebrew uses just one word, 'Hallelujah' for the three used in our English Bibles. Each verse of Psalm 150, except verse 6, starts with this word. Each verse is short because the psalmist, according to Spurgeon, 'is in haste to utter his next Hallelujah ... he is out of breath with enthusiasm ... as one on tiptoe, in the act of rising from earth to heaven.'[1] The psalmist uses only three or four words between each 'Praise the Lord' and uses five to introduce the 'Praise the Lord' in verse 6. The human author is unknown; this fact, however, is not important because the real focus of our adoration is the Lord.

Both the first and last psalms have six verses, but they are clearly different in scope: Psalm 1, the preface to the entire collection of the book of Psalms, describes the happiness of the person who loves and obeys God's word. Psalm 150 calls us to the enthusiastic worship of God and anticipates the eternal joy that awaits God's people.

The first three sections of the psalter end with 'Amen and Amen', which means 'let it be' (41:13; 72:19; 89:52); the last two sections conclude with 'Praise the Lord!' (106:48; 150:6).

Four questions will help us to explore this final psalm. May this study loosen our tongues to praise the Lord!

1. Whom do we praise?

We praise the Lord (vv. 1, 6): Jehovah/Yahweh, the 'I AM WHO I AM', the ever-present, eternal and unchanging covenant God who saves us and cares for us (Exod. 3:7–8, 14). The psalmist uses two names in the opening verse to describe the object of worship. He is, as we have seen, 'the Lord'; also referred to as 'God'. The Hebrew for this second name is 'El', which means 'the strong One'.

He is the Creator of 'his mighty heavens' (v. 1). The word translated as 'heavens' ('firmament', AV/NKJV) means 'an expanse, a thing spread out', and is used in Genesis 1:6–8: 'God said, "Let there be an expanse in the midst of the waters, and let it separate the waters from the waters" … and God called the expanse Heaven [sky]. And there was evening and there was morning, the second day'.

The heavens reveal God's splendour: 'The heavens declare the glory of God, and the sky above proclaims his handiwork' (Ps. 19:1). The apostle Paul also makes it clear that the existence of the created universe displays God's 'eternal power and divine nature' so that sinners have no excuse for their unbelief (Rom. 1:18–23).

So why don't non-Christians believe in God's existence, and adore him, when they see, for example, a beautiful sunset? The reason is because Satan has blinded their minds, so that they see, but do not see (1 Cor. 2:14; 2 Cor. 4:4). God by his Spirit, and through the Scriptures, opens the eyes of the spiritually blind (1 Cor. 2:8–10).

In the psalm just quoted, Psalm 19, David turns from looking at God's creation to consider God's word. God's word makes the simple wise: 'The testimony of the Lord is sure, making wise the simple' (Ps. 19:7), and giving sight to the blind: 'The commandment of the Lord is pure, enlightening the eyes' (Ps. 19:8). The Scriptures are like glasses that bring creation into focus.

2. Where do we praise?

The psalmist calls us to 'praise God in his sanctuary' (Ps. 150:1). Originally, the sanctuary was the temple in Jerusalem, the place of worship. In the Jewish mind the temple was also the dwelling place of God. However, Solomon at the dedication of the temple had prayed: 'But will God indeed dwell on the earth? Behold, heaven and the highest heaven cannot contain you' (1 Kings 8:27). God is far greater than we can ever understand.

As Christians we have no special sanctuary in some holy city. So how do these words apply to us? Perhaps the Septuagint (the Greek translation of the Old Testament) points us in the right direction when it translates 'in his sanctuary' as 'in his holy ones'. Believers are now God's temple (his sanctuary); he lives in them, his worshipping people. The apostles Paul and Peter both refer to the church as God's temple built on Christ 'the cornerstone' (2 Cor. 6:16–18; Eph. 2:19–22; 1 Peter 2:4–10). Similarly, the apostle John identifies 'the holy city, new Jerusalem' with 'a bride adorned for her husband' (Rev. 21:1–2; compare Eph. 5:25–27). The city/ bride is the church. The church is not the building where we worship but the people who worship God.

3. Why do we praise?

We praise God because he is worthy of our praise. We not only praise him for who he is, but also for what he has done. The psalmist celebrates 'his mighty deeds' and 'his excellent greatness' (v. 2). There are numerous examples in the Scriptures of God's 'mighty deeds', beginning with his creation of a vast universe in six days out of nothing by his spoken word (Gen. 1:1–31; 2:1–7; Ps. 33:4–9). Think also of his deliverance of his people, the Israelites, from Egyptian captivity and the miraculous crossing of the Red Sea (Exod. 12, 14–15). Moreover, not only did he preserve his people through their forty years in the wilderness wanderings but he also provided for them in all their needs (e.g., Exod. 16–17). Indeed, throughout the history of the Old Testament, God repeatedly saved the Jewish race from extermination at the hands of successive vicious enemies; not least among them being Haman, the Persian. The book of Esther tells the story of this deliverance.

Why was God so concerned for a nation that often offended him by their rebellion and idolatry? The ultimate answer is that from eternity he had decreed that from this race would emerge the Messiah, the Lord Jesus Christ, who is the Saviour of the world. The greatest display of the Lord's 'mighty deeds' was seen in Christ's death for sinners. The immortal God died on a cross! There he became the substitute for believing sinners; there he took their sins and the eternal punishment they deserved.

The phrase 'Praise him according to his excellent greatness!' (v. 2) means 'Praise him according to the abundance of his greatness.' It sadly reminds us that our praise, while on earth, is always inadequate. Matthew Henry comments: 'Our praises can [never] bear any proportion to God's greatness, for it is infinite, but since he is greater than we can express or conceive, we must raise our conceptions and expressions to the highest degree we can attain to. Be not afraid of saying too much in the praises of God, as we often do in praising even great and good men'.[2] Paul, citing Isaiah 40:13 and Job 41:11, praises God for his greatness in Romans 11:33–36. Adoration is the only response the apostle can make to the sovereignty of God in saving his elect—the subject of Romans 9–11.

4. How do we praise?

Old Testament believers praised the Lord with their voices and with the use of musical instruments. The variation in Bible versions indicate that the Hebrew scholars do not agree in their understanding of what these musical instruments were.

- Trumpet (v. 3). This was the blast from the ram's horn and was reserved for special occasions and for the giving of signals, rather than as an instrument for worship (eg. Lev. 25:9; 2 Sam. 15:10; 2 Chr. 15:14; Neh. 4:18–20; Ps. 81:3).
- Lute and harp (harp and lyre, NIV) (v. 3) were both small and hand-held framed instruments plucked with the fingers or with a plectrum. These two instruments were often used together (e.g. 1 Sam. 10:5; Ps. 33:2; 57:8).
- Tambourine and dance (v. 4). The tambourine or timbrel (NKJV) was a hand-held drum. Philip Eveson comments: 'It was an instrument used by women. It was played at banquets and other joyful social occasions (Isaiah 5:12; Jeremiah 31:4). There is no evidence it formed part of temple worship but it was used by the roaming prophets in their praises and at special religious functions outside the temple (1 Samuel 10:5; 2 Samuel 6:5; 1 Chronicles 13:8)'.[3] The 'dance' was probably some kind of pipe. Dancing in worship was exceptional, such as the dancing of Miriam and the women after crossing the Red Sea (Exod. 15:20–21), and David dancing when he brought the ark to Jerusalem (2 Sam. 6:1–15). These remarkable displays of God's power demanded extraordinary praise. There is no mention in the New Testament of dancing in worship.
- Strings and pipes (v. 4). The first term only occurs here; the pipes ('flutes', NKJV) only appear four times in the Old Testament (the other references being Gen. 4:21; Job 21:12; 30:31). There is no indication that the 'strings and pipes' were used in worship.
- Cymbals—the worshippers used two sorts of cymbals: sounding and clashing, one softer than the other. David used these when he brought the ark to Jerusalem. Paul refers to the clanging cymbal

in 1 Corinthians 13:1: 'If I speak in the tongues of men and of angels, but have not love, I am a noisy gong or a clanging cymbal.'

So now, we come to the controversial question of the use of musical instruments in worship today. Advocates for musical instruments often appeal to Psalm 150. Calvin taught that 'musical instruments belonged to the infancy of the church, nor should we foolishly imitate a practice which was intended only for God's ancient people.'[4] He emphatically affirms that musical instruments are no more useful in worship 'than the burning of incense, the lighting up of the lamps and the restoration of the other shadows of the law'.[5] Eveson shows that this is a flawed argument: 'While the ceremonial law and all the tabernacle furnishings are symbols of Christ and his priestly work, the same cannot be said of musical instruments. They are not used to symbolise anything but are like the suggested tunes, merely aids to singing the words.'[6]

As we consider this subject we ought to remember that Moses adhered strictly to God's commands in erecting the tabernacle (see for example Exod. 25:9, 40; 36:1), as did Solomon later, when he built the temple. God regulated every aspect of Jewish life and worship. The New Testament does not forbid, but neither does it encourage, the use of musical instruments in worship. There is no mention of their use in the early church. It is true that we read about harps in Revelation 5:8 (see also Rev. 14:2; 15:2), but the same verse speaks of 'golden bowls full of incense, which are the prayers of the saints'. If the 'golden bowls' are symbolic, the harps are too.

John Calvin (1509–1564) and Martin Luther (1483–1546) took different stances on what to allow and what to forbid in worship. Calvin: 'Anything not commanded in Scripture is forbidden.' Luther: 'Anything not forbidden in Scripture is permissible.' Theologians describe Calvin's view as 'the regulative principle' and Luther's as 'the normative principle'. Both Calvin and Luther emphasized the centrality of preaching in worship because it is through preaching that God saves sinners and sanctifies saints (Rom. 10:13–15; 1 Cor. 1:17–18, 21; 2 Tim. 3:14–17). The Puritans walked in the footsteps of Calvin; Anglicans adopted Luther's position.

If we follow 'the regulative principle' we ought to take care to distinguish between what God's word clearly teaches and what is part of our culture. Commenting on the subjects of worship and culture, Dr John Temple says: 'The Bible does not teach that a church in rural Africa or Asia must sing the same songs as may be sung in the UK or America. Nor are we bound to sing songs from another generation or genre. The elders must therefore carefully determine how their congregation can best express itself in truth and in music, while not crossing the line into entertainment ... nor merely imitating the world.'[7]

What then are the guiding principles for worship? In addition to enhancing God's glory, we ought to remember the apostle Paul's two exhortations, 'Let all things be done for building up' and, 'All things should be done decently and in order' (1 Cor.14:26, 40).

The emphasis of the new covenant is on the condition of the heart rather than on how or where we worship. Therefore, New Testament writers do not give detailed instructions about the format of worship. This stress on the heart is also found in the Old Testament (see for example Isa. 29:13) but becomes prominent in the New Testament. To quote Henry again: 'The best music in God's ears is devout and pious affections—not a melodious string, but a melodious heart.'[8] Henry echoes Paul when he speaks of 'making melody to the Lord with your heart' (Eph. 5:19 compare Col. 3:16).

Genuine worship, with or without musical accompaniment, must come from the heart. Paul highlights congregational singing rather than musical accompaniment, about which he says nothing in the verses already quoted from Ephesians and Colossians.

Jesus, in talking to a Samaritan woman, said: 'The hour ... is now here, when the true worshippers will worship the Father in spirit and in truth, for the Father is seeking such people to worship him. God is spirit, and those who worship him must worship in spirit and truth' (John 4:23–24). Perhaps with the intention of diverting our Lord from his probing comments about her personal life, the woman tries to focus attention on the most appropriate place of worship: a mountain in Samaria or the temple in Jerusalem. Jesus makes it abundantly plain that what really matters is not so much the place of worship as the attitude of our hearts and minds in worship. We must worship God 'in spirit and in truth'.

What is the meaning of 'spirit and truth'? To worship in 'spirit' is to offer sincere and wholehearted adoration to God; such worship is not rooted to holy places or confined to holy days. The Christian offering himself to God 'as a living sacrifice' presents to the Lord 'spiritual worship' (Rom.12:1). To worship in 'truth' is devotion that is in harmony with the clear teaching of God's Word. We need both 'spirit and truth' for balanced worship. Some commentators interpret 'spirit' as a reference to the Holy Spirit. It is only through God's Spirit that we offer to God acceptable worship.

The seventeenth-century Puritan, Stephen Charnock, in an exposition of John 4:24, takes the 'spirit' to mean the Holy Spirit: 'God is a Spirit infinitely happy, therefore we must approach him with cheerfulness; he is a Spirit of infinite majesty, therefore we come before him with reverence; he is infinitely high, therefore we must offer up sacrifices with deepest humility; he is infinitely holy, therefore we must address him with purity; he is infinitely glorious, we therefore must acknowledge his excellency ... he is a Spirit provoked by us, therefore we must offer up our worship in the name of a pacifying mediator and intercessor.'[9]

An eruption of praise

The psalm ends with a call for a universal torrent of praise: 'Let everything that has breath praise the Lord!' (v. 6). 'There is nothing in the Psalter more majestic or more beautiful than this brief but most significant finale.'[10] The praise of God's people on earth blends with that of angels and the redeemed who are already in heaven in anticipation of the never-ending adoration of God on the new earth, the final home of God's elect (Isa. 65:17–22; 66:22–23; 2 Peter 3:13).

What is the eternal theme of angels and saints? 'Worthy are you, our Lord and God, to receive glory and honour and power, for you created all things, and by your will they existed and were created ... Worthy is the Lamb who was slain, to receive power and wealth and wisdom and might and honour and glory and blessing!' (Rev. 4:11; 5:12). Meanwhile, we praise God in all circumstances, whether good or bad, rejoicing in the benediction promise of Jude 24: 'Now to him [God] who is able to keep you from stumbling and to present you blameless before the presence of his glory with great joy ...'

Chapter 15

NOTES

1   C. H. Spurgeon, *Treasury of David*, vol. 6 (repr. London: Marshall, Morgan & Scott, 1950), p.465.

2   Matthew Henry, *Commentary on the Whole Bible* (repr. Peabody, Massachusetts: Hendrickson, n.d.), p.954.

3   Philip Eveson, *Psalms*, vol. 2 (Welwyn Commentary; Darlington: Evangelical Press, 2015), p.506.

4   Calvin, *Commentary on the Psalms*, vol. 3 (Edinburgh: Calvin Translation Society, 1845; repr. Grand Rapids: Baker Book House, 1993), remarks on Psalm 149:3, p.539.

5   Calvin, *Commentary on the Psalms*, vol. 1 (Edinburgh: Calvin Translation Society, 1845; repr. Grand Rapids, Baker Book House, 1993), commenting on Psalm 33:2, p.539.

6   Eveson, *Psalms*, vol. 2, pp.510–511.

7   John Temple, *Bible-Centred Church—running a church the biblical way* (Leominster: Day One, 2001), pp.45–46.

8   Henry, *Commentary*, p.954.

9   Stephen Charnock, quoted by Erroll Hulse, *Who Are the Puritans?* (Darlington: Evangelical Press, 2000), p.21.

10   Joseph Addison Alexander, *Commentary on the Psalms* (Edinburgh: Andrew Elliot & James Thin, 1873), p.564.

Praise God for salvation

Behold, God is my salvation; I will trust, and will not be afraid; for the Lord GOD is my strength and my song, and he has become my salvation ... Shout, and sing for joy, O inhabitant of Zion, for great in your midst is the Holy One of Israel. (Isa. 12:2, 6)

Isaiah 12 reads like a psalm.[1] The prophet gives thanks and sings praises to God (vv. 1–2, 4–5). He urges his readers to 'Shout, and sing for joy' (v. 6). It is therefore an appropriate passage in a book on doxologies and benedictions.

What is the cause of this joy? Salvation! 'Behold God is my salvation ... he has become my salvation. With joy you will draw waters from the wells of salvation.' 'His deeds' (v. 4) and what he has 'done gloriously' (v. 5) must surely include salvation. God saves sinners—this fact sets this Jewish prophet singing! It should set us singing too!

A song about Christ

What does Isaiah mean by the phrase 'in that day' (vv. 1, 4)? It is the day that the prophet refers to in the previous chapter: 'In that day the root of Jesse, who shall stand as a signal for the peoples—of him shall the nations enquire, and his resting place shall be glorious' (Isa. 11:10). The opening verse of chapter 11 identifies 'the root of Jesse' (see also 4:2–6) as the 'branch', which is a description of the promised Messiah used several times in the Old Testament (Isa. 4:2; Jer. 23:5; 33:15; Zech. 3:8; 6:12; compare Rev. 5:5). God's people were like a decayed tree stump from which the Messiah would come. Paul quotes Isaiah 11:10 as a prophecy that God would call non-Jews, Gentiles, into his church (Rom. 15:12). The phrase 'a signal for the peoples' (Isa. 11:10) depicts Christ as a warrior carrying an unfurled banner, fighting alongside his troops, and leading them to victory.

God calling the Jews to return from exile in Babylon foreshadows the Lord saving sinners from all the nations of the world. His elect, Jews and Gentiles, are 'the remnant' (Isa. 11:11) that will ultimately comprise 'a great multitude that no one could number, from every nation, from all tribes and peoples and languages, standing before the throne and before the Lamb' (Rev. 7:9).

'In that day' means the time between Christ's first coming as a helpless baby at Bethlehem, and his second coming as the glorious King at the end of this world. The New Testament writers call this same period 'the last days' (Acts 2:17; 2 Tim. 3:1; Heb. 1:1–2).

A song about salvation

Who may sing this song? Those who can use the personal pronouns in verse 2: 'God is *my* salvation … *my* strength and *my* song … he has become *my* salvation' (emphasis added). This is the song of the saved! The saved have a personal experience of God's grace. Each one knows that God has forgiven his sins. Each one has turned from sin to trust Christ alone for salvation. Sadly, only a remnant, as predicted in Isaiah 6:13, just a stump of the nation's tree, praised God as their Saviour. Spiritual privileges such as birth into a Christian family or attendance at a place of worship do not guarantee salvation.

We often think of salvation as rescue or deliverance from sin and Satan. This is true, but salvation means much more. It is also reconciliation to an offended God. Look at how Isaiah begins his song: 'I will give thanks to you, O Lord, for though you were angry with me, your anger turned away, that you might comfort me' (v. 1). Sin, especially idolatry, was the reason for God's anger with his people.

Turning to the New Testament, we read that God is the enemy of the impenitent and that they are rebels against him. For example, we read in

Paul's letter to the Romans, 'For the wrath of God is revealed from heaven against all ungodliness and unrighteousness of men, who by their unrighteousness suppress the truth' (1:18); 'While we were enemies we were reconciled to God by the death of his Son' (5:10); 'The mind that is set on the flesh is hostile to God, for it does not submit to God's law; indeed, it cannot. Those who are in the flesh cannot please God' (8:7–8). 'The mind set on the flesh' is a description of unbelievers; this attitude leads to everlasting death. Believers live 'according to the Spirit'; they 'set their minds on the things of the Spirit'. This attitude leads to everlasting peace (8:5–6).

God's anger is 'turned away' (Isa. 12:1) from the penitent because his anger fell on Christ. God punished him instead of the repenting sinner: 'He was wounded for our transgressions; he was crushed for our iniquities; upon him was the chastisement that brought us peace, and with his stripes we are healed' (Isa. 53:5). To quote again from Romans: 'Since we have been justified by faith, we have peace with God through our Lord Jesus Christ'. God acquits us, he declares us not guilty—this is the meaning of justification. God pardons all who approach him through Christ; we have access, through him, into God's holy presence (Rom. 5:1–2). To know that God's anger is 'turned away' brings comfort to the soul: 'you … comfort me' (Isa. 12:1).

The name of God used by Isaiah tells us why he pardons his people: He is the 'Lord' (vv. 1, 4–5); he is 'The Lord God' (v. 2). The Hebrew is 'YAH, the Lord' and refers back to God speaking to Moses at the burning bush (Exod. 3:14). God delivered his enslaved people because of his covenant with Abraham. He heard their groaning and sent Moses as their deliverer (Exod. 2:23–25).

John MacArthur comments: 'The doubling of the personal name of God serves to emphasize His role as the covenant-keeping One.'[2] From eternity, God determined to save, through his Son's death, a vast number of sinners, from all nations and from all eras of history. All whom God chose and for whom Christ died will live for ever with him in heaven. God does not change his plans: therefore, he will never cease to love, and protect, his people.

A song of praise

God gives us *courage*: 'I will trust, and will not be afraid'; *strength*: 'God is my strength', and *joy*: 'God is ... my song' (v. 2). 'Trust' is confidence that God will save us—we are not afraid that he will reject us—and confidence that he will protect us. God will never fail us! This verse echoes Exodus 15:2, part of the song of Moses which we have considered in a previous chapter, and Psalm 118:14.

The Bible is full of stories about God giving his people courage, such as Noah building an ark to the sound of the ridicule of the ungodly (Gen. 6–8; 2 Peter 3:1–7); eighty-year-old Daniel facing the lions because he would not stop praying (Dan. 6); Esther pleading with the Persian king for the Jews threatened with extermination (Esther 4–5); and the apostles, who chose to obey God rather than men (Acts 5:29), with the result that most of them died as martyrs.

The emphasis of the words: 'God ... my strength' (Isa. 12:2) is that the Lord does more than give us strength. He himself is 'our complete strength; for we are strong, so far as he supplies us with strength'.[3] God our strength makes the weak strong: 'Have you not known? Have you not heard? The Lord is the everlasting God, the Creator of the ends of the earth. He does not faint or grow weary; his understanding is unsearchable. He gives power to the faint, and to him who has no might he increases strength. Even youths shall faint and be weary, and young men shall fall exhausted; but they who wait for the Lord shall renew their strength; they shall mount up with wings like eagles; they shall run and not be weary; they shall walk and not faint' (Isa.40:28–31). To 'wait for the Lord' is to obey God and to seek his guidance every day on the journey to heaven.

God is 'my song' because 'he has become my salvation' (v. 2). It is, 'with joy you will draw water from the wells of salvation' (v. 3). Water is a symbol which Isaiah uses often to describe the blessings of salvation (e.g. Isa. 41:17–18; 55:1, 10). God who gave the nomad Israelites water from the rock in the wilderness (Exod. 17) gives the water of everlasting life to those who come to him. Water is necessary for physical life; all that we need for spiritual life flows to us from God. Just as wells are deep, so there are depths to God's grace that we will never fathom. His mercy is deeper and greater than our sins. It never runs dry like human wells; rather it overflows like water from a fountain. We draw this water by trusting Christ alone for salvation. We draw water from this well whenever we ask for God's power to resist temptation and to cope with trials.

Jesus said to a Samaritan woman by Jacob's well: 'Everyone who drinks of this water will be thirsty again, but whoever drinks of the water that I will give him will never be thirsty again. The water that I will give him will become in him a spring of water welling up to eternal life' (John 4:13–14). At the Jewish feast of booths,[4] Jesus declared, 'If anyone thirsts, let him come to me and drink. Whoever believes in me, as the Scripture has said, "Out of his heart will flow rivers of living water." Now this he said about the Spirit, whom those who believed in him were to receive, for as yet the Spirit had not been given, because Jesus was not yet glorified' (John 7:37–39). To never thirst again denotes that Jesus bestows lasting satisfaction. He grants us eternal life even now while living on earth. 'Water welling up' and living rivers always flowing speak of God's inexhaustible grace and the permanent presence of God's Spirit in the heart.

The flowing water in John 7 may allude to the water mingled with wine that the priest poured from a golden pitcher on the sacrifice on the altar on the last day of the feast. The living water flows not from a huge water jug but from the heart of the believer. It overflows not on an altar but into the lives of others.

How should we respond to God's gifts of courage, strength and joy because of salvation? Isaiah 12:4 answers the question. We give to him more praise: 'Give thanks to the Lord'; we pray: 'call upon his name'; and we proclaim to everyone what he has done: 'make known his deeds among the peoples, proclaim that his name is exalted'. Verses 5–6 also take up the refrain of singing and shouting for joy. We cannot keep quiet about our glorious Saviour! A joyless Christian is someone who does not enjoy God as his Saviour!

A song about Zion

Verse 6 depicts Zion as a woman whom Isaiah commands to shout in celebration of the Lord's greatness. God, who does not need our praise, gives us the honour of extolling the glory of his name!

Isaiah calls each of the saved an 'inhabitant of Zion' (v. 6). Zion, a name for Jerusalem, became a collective title for the entire nation. Paul calls believers 'the Israel of God' (Gal. 6:16). The writer to the Hebrews affirms that believers 'have [now] come to Mount Zion and to the city of the living God, the heavenly Jerusalem' (Heb. 12:22). We belong to an unshakeable city in contrast to the earthly Jerusalem that was destroyed many times (Heb. 12:27). 'Inhabitant' is a feminine word in the Hebrew and reminds us that the church is the bride of Christ (Eph. 5:23; Rev. 19:7; 21:2, 9).

God the great King, the Holy One of Israel, lives among his people (v. 6). He is Immanuel—God with us—whose incarnation Isaiah announced some seven hundred years before the event (Isa. 7:14; 9:6–7; Matt. 1:22–23). The apostle John, exiled to the Greek island of Patmos because of his faithfulness to Christ, wrote, 'I heard a loud voice from the throne saying, "Behold, the dwelling place of God is with man. He will dwell with them, and they will be his people, and God himself will be with them as their God.

He will wipe away every tear from their eyes, and death shall be no more, neither shall there be mourning, nor crying, nor pain any more, for the former things have passed away"' (Rev. 21:3–4).

Meanwhile God lives in the temple of his people: 'we are the temple of the living God; as God said, "I will make my dwelling among them and walk among them, and I will be their God, and they shall be my people"' (2 Cor. 6:16; see also 1 Cor. 6:19). Paul's message is this: holy living is the evidence and the outcome of God living, by his Spirit, within his people.

Who are the inhabitants of this city? Only those who can sincerely say, 'God is my salvation' (v. 2); the door into this city is Christ-centred and cross-shaped. Have you come, in repentance and faith, to the Lord Jesus Christ, who said, 'I am the door. If anyone enters by me, he will be saved' (John 10:9)?

The word 'Behold' (v. 2) expresses the prophet's excitement and amazement at God's saving grace. Are you excited when you think about salvation?

Chapter 16

NOTES

1   Derek Thomas divides Isaiah 12 into two songs (vv.1–3; vv.4–6). *God Delivers* (Welwyn Commentary; Darlington: Evangelical Press, 1991), p.114.

2   John MacArthur, *The MacArthur Study Bible NKJV* (Dallas: Word Publishing, 1997), p.297 (note on Isaiah 12:2).

3   John Calvin, *Commentary on the Book of Isaiah*, vol. 1 (Edinburgh: Calvin Translation Society; repr. Grand Rapids: Baker Book House, 1993), p.400.

4   The feast of booths or tabernacles reminded the Jews of their forefathers living in tents for forty years in the wilderness at the time of Moses.

A prophet's benediction

Blessed be the name of God for ever and ever ... To you, O God of my fathers, I give thanks and praise. (Dan. 2:20, 23)

C an you hear marching boots? They belong to the armies of Nebuchadnezzar marching into Jerusalem in 605 BC. A young Daniel sees the soldiers devastating Jerusalem, the capital city of Judah. Soon his feet are sore as the soldiers force him to walk over a thousand miles to Babylon. Over a period of twenty-three years Nebuchadnezzar deported most of Judah's population to Babylon, in what is now known as Iraq.

Promises

Daniel and his friends, Shadrach, Meshach and Abednego, remained loyal to God. They remembered God's promise of a return to their homeland. They looked further ahead and recalled God's promise of a coming Messiah-Saviour. They risked their lives rather than disobey God. The Lord stood with courageous Shadrach, Meshach and Abednego in the fire (Dan. 3) and shut the mouths of lions to protect a brave eighty-year-old Daniel (Dan. 6).

Piety

Daniel's godliness was evident to everyone, including his malicious enemies, who 'could find no ground for complaint or any fault [in him], because he was faithful, and no error or fault was found in him' (Dan. 6:4). What was the source of Daniel's lifelong godliness? He read God's Word. We read that Daniel 'perceived in the books' (Dan. 9:2) that the time of the seventy-year exile was almost at an end. He studied the prophecy of Jeremiah (Dan. 9:2) and 'the Law of Moses' (Dan. 9:13). Having read God's Word he prayed: 'Then I turned my face to the Lord God, seeking him by prayer ... I prayed to the Lord my God and made confession' (Dan. 9:3–4). He asked God to fulfil his promises and to forgive the nation's sins. It is unmistakable from Daniel's prayer that he had saturated his mind with Scripture.

Prayer

Moreover, it is clear from the book of Daniel that, throughout his life, he was a man of prayer. His penitential prayer in chapter 9 is one of the greatest prayers recorded in the Bible. We read in earlier chapters about Daniel praying to interpret Nebuchadnezzar's strange dream (2:17–19) and praying when enemies plotted against him. We read that 'when Daniel knew that the document [commanding exclusive and idolatrous worship of the king] had been signed, he went to his house ... He got down on his knees three times a day and prayed and gave thanks before his God, as he had done previously' (6:10). He had only to stop praying to God and to offer petitions to king Darius for thirty days (6:7). The stark choice was between life and death. To stop praying meant prolonged life; to keep praying could lead to a painful death in the lions' den. But for Daniel, there really was no choice; he must pray to the one true and living God whatever the consequences of doing so might be. His undoubted godliness grew from the soil of God's Word and prayer.

Praise

In addition to reading God's Word and praying three times a day, Daniel praised God, 'He ... prayed and gave thanks before his God' (6:10). The fearless prophet praises even though he might provide a tasty meal for hungry lions!

In the second chapter of his prophecy we read Daniel's benediction in which he praises God (Dan. 2:20–23). What events prompted this benediction? A king's nightmare which he couldn't get out of his mind and which none of his wise men could describe or explain. The king was Nebuchadnezzar in the second year of his reign. What was his dream? He saw a massive dazzling statue of a man with a gold head, chest and arms of silver, belly and thighs made of bronze, and with legs of iron and toes of clay, destroyed by a stone which grows to the size of a mountain.

The king refused to relate his dream but demanded an explanation. 'It's impossible to interpret the dream without knowing what it was', reply the wise men. 'Explain or I will put you to death!' shouts the angry monarch. This death sentence included Daniel, Shadrach, Meshach and Abednego, who had been educated by the wisest men in Babylon.

Daniel's response to this news was to ask Nebuchadnezzar for time to reveal and interpret the dream. Then, together with his three friends, he prays that the merciful God would make known the king's dream and its meaning. Solomon, Israel's third king, renowned for his wisdom, wrote: 'The Lord gives wisdom; from his mouth come knowledge and understanding' (Prov. 2:6). That night Daniel had a vision and he 'blessed the God of heaven' who had answered his prayer.

Daniel is careful to exalt the all-wise God who gave the dream to the king and who had explained it to him (v. 28). The dream was an unfolding of history: the image represented four world powers: the Babylonian, replaced by the Persian, followed by the Greek, and later the Roman Empire. The metals become of lesser importance, signifying the decreasing power of the kingdoms. The king also saw in his dream a kingdom set up by God and depicted as a stone as vast as a mountain that destroys all human kingdoms but is never itself destroyed. The stone is Christ; the indestructible kingdom is the everlasting kingdom of God (vv. 31–45).

In his benediction Daniel highlights several aspects of God's 'name' (v. 20)—a term which sums up all that God has told us about himself in the Scriptures. This benediction is a model of how we ought to praise God.

He is the sovereign 'God of heaven' (vv. 18–19), to whom belongs 'might' (v. 20). He is the one who 'changes times and seasons; he removes kings and set up kings' (v. 21). It is not Nebuchadnezzar who is 'king of kings' but 'the God of heaven'. God, who made the universe, and who rules the nations of the world, gave to him 'the kingdom, the power, and the might, and the glory' (v. 37). The only reason he was on the throne of Babylon was because God had placed him there.

The interpretation of the king's dream affirms that nothing happens apart from God's decree. He knows all events because he plans them. This fact humbled proud Nebuchadnezzar (vv. 46–49), but his humility was short lived. Soon he built an enormous gold image of himself which everyone must worship (Dan. 3:1–7). Perhaps it was the 'great image' (Dan. 2:31) seen in his mysterious dream that suggested the idea to the conceited king. God warned the arrogant monarch in a second dream of imminent judgment if he refused to repent (4:4–27). His boasting shows that he ignored this threat: '"Is not this great Babylon, which I have built by my mighty power …?" While the words were still in the king's mouth, there fell a voice from heaven, "O King Nebuchadnezzar, to you it is spoken: The kingdom has departed from you, and you shall be driven from among men, and your dwelling shall be with the beasts of the field … until you know that the Most High rules the kingdom of men and gives it to whom he will"' (4:28–32). After seven years the restored king declared God's sovereignty (4:34–37). He learnt the hard way that 'the Most High rules.'

Darius, the Persian king, was also compelled to acknowledge God's sovereignty after the incident of Daniel and the lion's den (Dan. 6:25–27). Both these defiant rulers discovered that before God 'the inhabitants of the earth are accounted as nothing, and he does according to his will among the host of heaven and among the inhabitants of the earth; and none can stay his hand or say to him, "What have you done?"' (Dan. 4:35).

He is the eternal God who will receive adoration 'for ever and ever'

(Dan. 2:20). The wise men desire that Nebuchadnezzar the king will live for ever (Dan. 2:4). For all his might, 'The king is simply another passing phase in the wobbly annals of international royal governments.'[1] God alone is eternal. He is 'the Most High … who lives forever', whose 'dominion is an everlasting dominion, and his kingdom endures from generation to generation' (Dan. 4:34). He is 'the Ancient of Days' who gives to 'one like a son of man' (Christ) 'dominion and glory and a kingdom, that all peoples, nations, and languages should serve him; his dominion is an everlasting dominion, which shall not pass away, and his kingdom one that shall not be destroyed' (Dan. 7:9–14; Rev. 7:9–12). The description 'Ancient of Days' means that he is the uncreated and everlasting God in contrast to the mortal monarchs and rulers of earthly kingdoms.

He is the God 'to whom belong[s] wisdom' (Dan. 2:20). It is God who 'gives wisdom to the wise and knowledge to those who have understanding' and who 'reveals deep and hidden things' (vv. 21–22). The wise God 'knows what is in the darkness'—nothing is hidden from him—and 'the light dwells with him' (v. 22)—he knows all things. God gave Daniel wisdom to know the content and the meaning of Nebuchadnezzar's disturbing dream (v. 23).

The word 'light' (v. 22) brings to mind Paul's words to Timothy concerning God, 'the blessed and only Sovereign, the King of kings and Lord of lords, who alone has immortality, who dwells in unapproachable light, whom no one has ever seen or can see. To him be honour and eternal dominion. Amen' (1 Tim. 6:15–16). The invisible and unapproachable God becomes visible and approachable in God the Son, the Lord Jesus Christ (John 1:18; 14:8–11; 2 Cor. 4:6; Eph. 2:18). We enjoy fellowship with God who is light because 'the blood of Jesus his Son cleanses us from all sin' (1 John 1:5–9).

The generous Lord delights to give wisdom to those who ask him (James 1:5–8; 17). The rulers of this world are too proud to pray for divine wisdom, but God reveals himself to the humble. The apostle Paul, who contrasts human wisdom and God's wisdom, quotes Isaiah the prophet (Isa. 64:4): '"What no eye has seen, nor ear heard, nor the heart of man imagined, [is] what God has prepared for those who love him"— these things God has revealed to us through the Spirit. For the Spirit searches everything, even the depths of God' (1 Cor. 2:6–11). Believers are wiser than the cleverest unbelievers! What we shall know, when Christ returns, of 'the depths of God' is beyond our imagination!

He is the gracious God of the covenant. Daniel adores the 'God of my fathers' (v. 23). The exclamation 'O' indicates his intensity. The covenant God chose first Abraham and then, from his descendants, formed the nation of Israel from which the Messiah was born. In Christ were fulfilled those promises of God to Abraham which were destined to encircle the entire globe! Jesus is the Saviour of the world. Messiah's coming hinged on the faithful God saving his people from destruction.

Promotion

As promised to the interpreter of his dream (Dan. 2:6), Nebuchadnezzar 'gave Daniel high honours and many great gifts, and made him ruler over the whole province of Babylon and chief prefect over all the wise men of Babylon' (v. 48). Daniel graciously put in a good word for his three friends, Shadrach, Meshach and Abednego (v. 49), who prayed with him (vv. 17–18). These four men faithfully served the divine Master as they worked for the welfare of their temporary home in Babylon.

The sovereign, eternal and wise God who gave a pagan king a glimpse of future events has planned your future and mine! The God 'who knows what is in the darkness' (v. 22) will be with us when we walk through dark valleys. 'You can walk into the future with a God like that—who shows you that history is going toward his unshakable kingdom and who assures you that even though you have many personal uncertainties you follow a God who knows what is in the darkness. So you can keep going with hope and without fear.'[2]

Chapter 17

NOTES

1   Dale Ralph Davis, *The Message of Daniel* (The Bible Speaks Today; Nottingham: Inter-Varsity Press, 2013), p.39.

2   Davis, *Message of Daniel*, p.45.

Praise God on bad days

I will rejoice in the Lord; I will take joy in the God of my salvation. God, the Lord, is my strength. (Hab. 3:18–19)

The phrase in the heading of Habakkuk 3, 'according to Shigionoth', was probably a musical or liturgical term; it only occurs here and in the heading of Psalm 7. Habakkuk's prayer was also a song of praise, accompanied 'with stringed instruments' (v. 19). The word 'Selah',[1] which is used over seventy times in the book of Psalms, occurs three times here (vv. 3, 9, 13). This chapter is, therefore, suitable for a book on doxologies. We are going to concentrate on the closing verses.

What is the theme of Habakkuk? The end of chapter 2:4 provides the answer: 'The righteous shall live by his faith.' Bearing this verse in mind, we may divide the book into three parts as follows:

- Chapter 1—faith tested
- Chapter 2—faith taught
- Chapter 3—faith triumphant

'Whatever happens I will rejoice in the Lord', affirms Habakkuk in the closing verses of his prophecy.

Nineteenth-century Scotsman, Alexander MacLaren, calls chapter 3 'one of the most magnificent pieces of imaginative poetry in Scripture or anywhere else'.[2]

The trembling prophet (v. 16)

What made Habakkuk's body tremble and his lips quiver? Bad news! Who gave this bad news to the prophet? God! And what was the bad news? 'The cruel and depraved Chaldeans will take my people into

Babylon.' Why did God allow the Jews, his own people, to suffer? It was because of their sinful behaviour.

Habakkuk honestly tells us how he feels. Believers, with genuine faith and living obedient lives, have often struggled with doubts and fears as tears flowed down their faces. It is encouraging to realise that Habakkuk, like Elijah, 'was a man with a nature like ours' (James 5:17).

The prophet says that 'rottenness enters into my bones' (v. 16). He felt sapped of energy and strength. Does God condemn Habakkuk? Not at all! God, who is our heavenly Father, understands, and makes allowances for, our human weaknesses (Ps. 103:13–14). The psalmist in Psalm 103 writes about God's compassion to those who 'fear him'. This 'fear' is not that of a child who is frightened of an abusive parent; it is rather the fear of love and adoration. God is our Father, but he is also holy: therefore, we should fear lest we offend him. The words 'he knows our frame' in Psalm 103 refer to our emotions, our psychological make-up, rather than our physical bodies. A wise father or mother makes a distinction between what is naughty and what is childish behaviour. For example, a defiant child receives discipline; a child afraid of a dog or the dark needs understanding. God is wiser and kinder than the best human father.

How does Habakkuk cope with his reaction to bad news? He recalls God's mighty power, for example, in parting the Red Sea so that the Israelites escaped from the pursuing Egyptians (vv. 8–10; Exod. 14). God also made the sun stand still so that Israel might triumph (v. 11; Josh. 10). The almighty God can bring good things out of bad days.

After recalling examples of God's power Habakkuk says: 'I will quietly wait for the day of trouble to come upon people who invade us' (v. 16). The prophet waits patiently in God's presence. What is he waiting for? For God to come to the 'people'. This could mean his own sinful people, the Jews, or the Chaldeans. The important point, however we interpret the end of verse 16, is that Habakkuk is consciously bringing his problem to God. Furthermore, he is waiting for God to fulfil his Word. What should we do when we receive bad news? Pray and remember God's power and rest on his promises.

The triumphant prophet (vv. 17–19)

The trembling prophet becomes the triumphant prophet when he turns his thoughts away from the bad news to the good God.

Habakkuk imagines the worst things that could happen in verse 17: 'Though the fig tree should not blossom, nor fruit be on the vines, the produce of the olive fail and the fields yield no food, the flock be cut off from the fold and there be no herd in the stalls, yet I will rejoice in the Lord'. Failure of the crops and the death of livestock would be a nightmare for an agricultural nation. All this did happen, and worse, when the Chaldeans marched into Judah.

What is the worst that you could imagine? The death of husband or wife; the abduction of a son or daughter; an accident that leaves you severely disabled or mentally disturbed; a specialist saying, 'you have only a few weeks to live'; your home and possessions destroyed by flood or fire. Would you—would I—still praise our God?

In verse 18, 'Yet I will rejoice in the Lord; I will take joy in the God of my salvation', Habakkuk is saying, 'On the worst day of my life, I will still praise my God.' What reasons do we have for praising God on such a day?

We can rejoice on bad days …

1. Because God cares for us.

He is the 'Lord' (v. 18) who heard the cries of his afflicted people enslaved in Egypt and sent Moses to deliver them (Exod. 2:23–25; 3:7–8, 14). On the blackest day of our life, he will still be our God who loves us. There is no calamity that can separate the believer from God's love (Rom. 8:35–39).

2. Because God plans for us.

He is the 'Lord'—the sovereign God who wisely and lovingly plans every event in the life of each one of his children. Nothing can happen that he has not planned. No situation can arise that will take him by surprise. Think again of the familiar words of Romans 8:28: 'We know that for those who love God all things work together for good, for those who are called according to his purpose.'

3. Because God saves us

'I will take joy in the God of my salvation' (v. 18). 'Salvation' means 'deliverance'. After seventy years God delivered his people from exile in Babylon. I think that Habakkuk has a greater deliverance in mind—deliverance from sin. We can know more about this deliverance than Habakkuk, who lived some 600 years before Christ. In the awful moments of our lives we ought to remember Romans 8:32: 'He who did not spare his own Son but gave him up for us all, how will he not also with him graciously give us all things?' The God who planned 'all things' (Rom. 8:28) will also give us 'all things' (Rom. 8:32) necessary for our homeward journey towards heaven. He who saved our immortal souls will also care for our 'lowly body' and finally transform it 'to be like his glorious body' (Phil. 3:21).

4. Because our joy is centred on, and comes from, the Lord

'I will take joy in ... God' (v. 18). Nineteenth-century Hebrew scholars, Keil and Delitzsch, comment: 'God is the inexhaustible source and infinite sphere of the joy, because He is the God of salvation, and rises up to judgment upon the nations, to procure the salvation of His people.'[3]

Our joy does not depend on changing circumstances, whether good or bad, but on the immutable God, whose love towards us never changes. Nothing and no one can take God away from us. Nothing and no one can take us away from God. When all is gone, our God has not gone: he is always with us.

We should notice Habakkuk's determination to rejoice expressed in the words: 'I will …' (v. 18). This God has not failed us in the past. He will not fail us today or tomorrow, whatever the future holds. This inward joy overcomes all fears, terrors, sorrows and anxieties.

5. Because God gives us strength

'GOD, the Lord, is my strength' (v. 19). 'The Lord God is my Strength, my personal bravery, and my invincible army' (Amplified Bible). He makes the weak strong. He gives us the swift feet of the deer to run to him. He helps us to climb away from the predator, like a deer, into the safe hills of his protecting love and mercy: 'He makes my feet like the deer's; he makes me tread on my high places' (v. 19).

The believer can say with Paul, 'I can do all things through him who strengthens me' (Phil. 4:13). He was in a Roman prison when he wrote these words! Through Christ's strength we may move from trembling fear to triumphant faith.

Praising God

Is it really possible to praise God on bad days? Yes it is! Joni Eareckson Tada, a quadriplegic, writes: 'A man who recently lost his wife to breast cancer took comfort that, while his prayer wasn't granted, another prayer *was* answered'—the prayer of our Saviour, 'Father, I want those you have given me to be with me where I am, and to see my glory' (John 17:24, NIV). Joni comments: 'It's the heartfelt prayer of God's Son for all those who love Him. So the length of time we live on earth or whether or not we get healed isn't really the point, is it? The point is, we're all headed for heaven—the place where in the end Jesus wants us to be.'[4] There we will adore him with perfect praise!

Chapter 18

1 John Calvin, *Commentaries on the Minor Prophets*, vol. 4 (Edinburgh: Calvin Translation Society; repr. Grand Rapids: Baker Book House, 1993), p.165: 'The word [Selah] means to raise or to elevate; and it was therefore put down to remind the singers to raise their voice'. Some scholars think that 'Selah' means a pause in the singing. The precise meaning of the word is unknown.

2 Alexander MacLaren, *Expositions of Holy Scripture: Old Testament*, (electronic edition STEP Files © 2006).

3 C. F. Keil and F. Delitzsch, *Commentary on the Old Testament*, vol. 10, (repr. Peabody, Massachusetts: Hendrickson, 1989) p.15.

4 Joni Eareckson Tada, *A Spectacle of Glory—God's light shining through me every day* (Grand Rapids: Zondervan, 2016), p.90—the reading for March 17.